LEADING A DEPARTMENT

—— TRAINING GUIDE ——

Developing the Character and Competency
to Lead a Ministry

Mac Lake

MOVEMENTS
PUBLISHING

First published in 2022 by 100 Movements Publishing

Copyright © 2022 by Mac Lake

All rights reserved. No portion of this book may be reproduced or transmitted in any form or by any means, electronic or mechanical, including photocopying, recording, or by any information storage and retrieval system, without permission in writing from the author. The only exception is brief quotations in printed reviews.

The author has no responsibility for the persistence or accuracy of URLs for external or third-party internet websites referred to in this book, and does not guarantee that any content on such websites is, or will remain, accurate or appropriate.

All Scripture quotations, unless otherwise indicated, are taken from the Holy Bible, New International Version®, NIV®. Copyright ©1973, 1978, 1984, 2011 by Biblica, Inc.™ Used by permission of Zondervan. All rights reserved worldwide. www.zondervan.com. The "NIV" and "New International Version" are trademarks registered in the United States Patent and Trademark Office by Biblica, Inc.™

Scripture quotations marked NLT are taken from the Holy Bible, New Living Translation, copyright ©1996, 2004, 2015 by Tyndale House Foundation. Used by permission of Tyndale House Publishers, Inc., Carol Stream, Illinois 60188. All rights reserved.

ISBN 978-1-955142-17-5 (print)
ISBN 978-1-955142-18-2 (ebook)

100 Movements Publishing
An imprint of Movement Leaders Collective
Cody, Wyoming

www.100Mpublishing.com
www.movementleaderscollective.com
www.catalysechange.org

To Ken

Contents

Preface

Welcome to *Leading a Department: Developing the Character and Competency to Lead a Ministry*. This is your opportunity to advance in your development so that you learn both the character and the competency necessary to effectively lead a ministry, such as a children's, student, worship, or outreach ministry. This particular book in the Discipling Leaders Series can be used to help develop you as a volunteer or a paid staff member to lead a ministry department within your church. I recommend you first complete the prior books in the series in order to gain the competencies at the previous leadership levels.

I've dreamed of writing this type of training book for years, because so much training material focuses either on leadership competencies *or* on the character of the leader. Over the years I've watched leaders grow in their leadership but then be "taken out" because of a flaw in their character. Conversely, I've seen leaders who are godly men or women but are unable to mobilize people because of a lack of leadership competency.

As we develop leaders, we must help them grow in both character *and* competency. One of my favorite Bible verses is Psalm 78:72: "David shepherded them with integrity of heart; with skillful hands he led them." David was a great leader because he had both leadership skills and leadership spirit. When a leader has both, he or she is able to unite people and mobilize them to make a kingdom impact.

So I wanted to provide something that helps leaders grow in both character and competency.

The Discipling Leaders Series is a training resource for churches that are building a pipeline to draw new leaders from within and develop them along an intentional pathway of personal and professional growth. Each level of the Leadership Pipeline corresponds to a broader scope of responsibility and greater spiritual maturity.

Leading The Church

Leading Departments

Leading Leaders

Leading Others

Leading Self

The Leadership Pipeline in a church begins with leading self. This is where the majority of people will be in the average congregation. Most churches utilize small groups, Sunday School, or one-on-one mentoring to disciple those who are learning to lead themselves. Although this is a critical step in every believer's journey, the scope of this series is not about leading yourself. In my experience, many churches struggle with the discipleship of leaders. Therefore, this series focuses on how to disciple leaders at the various levels of the pipeline in the church.

Leading A Department is the third book in the Discipling Leaders Series. Each level has specific skill sets and character traits that must be mastered in order to have a full range of expertise before moving to another leadership level:

Leading Others
Leading Leaders
Leading a Department
Leading the Church

I've discovered that most organizations structure for function but never think about structuring for development. The Leadership Pipeline framework gives a strategy for developing leaders from within a church rather than having to hire externally. We have often defaulted to the easy route of "buying" leaders from the outside rather than building leaders from within. The Discipling Leaders Series helps equip those who have the call, the character, and the competencies to move to new levels of leadership. (You can learn more about building a Leadership Pipeline for your church or organization in one of my previous books, *The Multiplication Effect,* or by contacting me at multiplygroup.org.)

I am thankful for the encouragement and support of so many on the journey to publishing this book. I want to thank my wife, Cindy, who keeps a constant flow of encouraging words coming my way, fueling my soul when I get tired of writing and want to give up (not to mention the constant flow of coffee and healthy snacks she brings to keep my mind and body strong and alert). Thank you to Matt Rogers, an incredible writer who helped push me to finish this book. His partnership brought *Leading a Department* to a different level. And thank you to all the churches that have been through the Leadership Pipeline training process and encouraged me to write these training modules.

I hope you enjoy this journey.

Mac Lake

Before You Begin

What Makes This Training Guide Unique?

1. An Apprenticeship Approach

This training requires the assistance and accountability of a trainer, normally someone your church leadership designates. Although you will work through the content of each module on your own, you will discuss your responses and reflections with a trainer. The trainer functions as both a mentor and a model of the core character traits and competencies needed to develop the next level of leadership. You will learn and grow under their leadership as they observe your strengths and speak into your specific growth areas. In each module you will be required to put into practice the principles you're learning. The trainer will give you opportunities to practice in the context of their leadership role and ministry by sharing some responsibilities and leadership tasks with you—it is intended to be an apprenticeship approach to your development. In fact, this guide can be worked through with up to two others meeting with you and your trainer as a small learning cohort. Having other learners beside you in the process will significantly increase your learning as together you discuss your insights and discoveries along the way. This team approach is a return to the ancient form of mentoring that Jesus used with his disciples.

TRAINER: Please see **For the Trainer** on page 221.

2. A Focus on Character and Competency

In each module, the focus is on two elements of leadership: deepening your *character* and developing your *competency*. The principle behind this structure is to develop the skills of a leader in sync with the soul of a true leader. When you operate both in tandem, your character can accommodate the acquisition of skills and can execute them in a godly manner that honors the principles taught in God's Word.

What Is the Philosophy of This Training?

This training is designed to produce transformation in your skills, not just help you absorb information. Lots of time and thought went into the structure of this material. I believe transformation happens in a triad of development with three overlapping factors.

1. Knowledge

In order to develop specific competencies, you need to learn key information about how to actually do the associated skills.

For example, if I wanted to improve my golf swing, I could buy a golf magazine featuring an article on five steps to the perfect swing. After reading and digesting the information, does it improve my swing? Not really. It does, however, give me some good information on the skills of a good swing.

2. Experience

If you want to experience transformation in your leadership character or competencies, you must put that competency into practice. That's where learning really begins to accelerate. It's the experience that allows you to see where you're strong and where you need to grow. It's practice that produces failure and frustration, and that's a good thing because it raises questions, which then leads to greater learning.

Practice can also lead to success, which produces greater levels of learning and confidence in that particular leadership skill.

Let's go back to my golf example. I'm trying to improve my golf swing. I read the article on the five steps to the perfect golf swing. That gives me the knowledge. But then I need experience. So I grab a nine iron, go to my backyard, and swing a thousand times. Now, does that improve my swing? Not necessarily. If I'm doing things the right way, I may improve. But it may make things worse if I'm swinging incorrectly. When I make the same mistake repeatedly, I am reinforcing a bad habit.

3. Coaching

In order to develop your leadership competencies, you also need someone to observe you in action, give you feedback, and discuss what you are learning in the process. The coaching portion is where learning is solidified. The trainer/coach can give further assignments, which can lead to further practice, which will lead to further growth.

Once again, let's go back to improving my golf swing. So far I have read the article and practiced my swing in my backyard. Now I'm going to invite my friend who's a golf pro to come and observe my swing and give me feedback. As he's watching, he says, "Whoa, whoa, wait a minute, Mac. Keep your head down. Hold on, keep your left arm straight. Bend those knees." As he gives me this feedback, my swing begins to improve, new habits are developed, and eventually I produce a nice swing that enables me to lower my score by seven strokes. Success!

The focus is on *transformation*, not just the exchange of information. When you practice all three of these elements on a consistent basis, then you see transformation really start to happen.

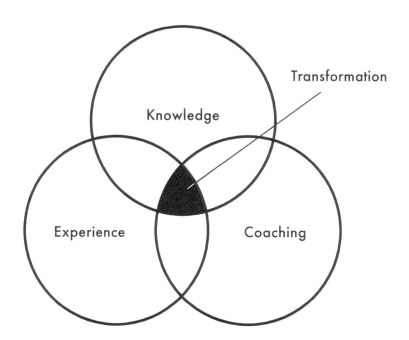

How Do I Get the Most Out of These Modules?

You may have previously participated in leadership training and at the time thought it was really great. Yet a few days later, you're unsure how to apply what you've learned or simply can't remember it. To ensure this is not your experience here, follow these tips:

- Work through the content of the module on your own, making sure you have enough time and headspace to engage with the questions fully. Write your answers and thoughts in the spaces provided throughout the modules.
- Don't just read the "Put It Into Practice" section. Take it seriously and recognize that the practice of the skill is what will help you grow in that area. Take every opportunity to practice what you are learning, whether in your home, work, or church context. This practice will sharpen your skill and build your leadership confidence.

- Every other week, meet with your trainer and up to two other trainees to discuss your reflections. Come to each session ready to share what you learned from the reading and from putting this skill into practice. Your trainer is someone who is experienced at leading others and can give you feedback, insights, and ideas that will better equip you to do the same.

- Shadow your trainer as they lead in their ministry area. Following them around, attending a huddle they are leading, or watching them engage one-on-one with one of their leaders can be a valuable learning experience as they model healthy leadership to you.

How Long Will the Training Take?

One of the first questions people ask is "How long will it take me to finish this training?" However, the goal is not to "finish" or "get through" the training. The goal is shaping your character and competencies as a leader. Some people will learn and adapt quickly. Others will require more time and practice. Ideally, you can take up to two weeks to complete each module. Meet with your trainer every other week. But don't rush. And don't cram. Pace yourself as a learner to digest the material and put it into practice.

Because *Leading a Department* is a discipleship-based training rather than a traditional classroom-based training, there is a flexible timeline for you to complete each module. In other words, this mentoring-/discipleship-based approach means you may or may not cover one module in one meeting. You and your trainer may choose to spend several meetings on one topic to ensure you're developing the character and competency for that module. The objective is to demonstrate growth, not just absorb the information.

How Is Each Module Organized?

The modules are very interactive and will require you to write down your answers and reflections. Each module includes various sections that will help you learn more rapidly, including:

■ Learning Objectives

Focus points to learn as a result of this study. Though you may gain additional learning from the modules, the objectives are designed to guide you to these particular outcomes.

■ Preassessment

A self-diagnostic to assess your current character and competency before you begin a module.

■ Deepen Your Character

A study from Scripture on a character trait that undergirds each competency. The study includes questions that help you process the information and spark transformative discussion.

■ Develop Your Competency

Content about how to develop a particular competency, with follow-up questions.

■ Put It Into Practice

Assignments to complete and/or review with your trainer.

■ Reflect on Your Learning

Questions to help you grasp your key takeaways from the module.

Now that you understand the uniqueness of this training and have a big picture overview, let's dive in and get started.

Overview of Modules

In *Leading a Department*, you will develop your competencies and grow in your character traits by completing these modules:

Module 1: Personal Development

Character: *Self-Awareness*
Leaders are keenly aware and honest about how their emotional and behavioral tendencies impact those around them.

Competency: *Personal Development*
Continuously pursue learning opportunities to gain new insights and wisdom that enable growth in character and leadership competencies.

Module 2: Time Management

Character: *Self-Discipline*
Leaders yield to the Holy Spirit, making the right decisions despite their emotions and temptations.

Competency: *Time Management*
Steward time in a wise manner that minimizes distractions and maximizes personal contribution to the organization's mission.

Module 3: Decision Making

Character: *Discernment*
Leaders recognize and respond to the presence and activity of God.

Competency: *Making Decisions*
Weigh a variety of options to make a prayerful, wise choice that reflects God's desired outcome.

Module 4: Communication

Character: *Authenticity*
Leaders acknowledge they are broken and imperfect while trusting God's grace and his Spirit to conform them to the image of Christ.

Competency: *Communication*
Communicate clearly so others understand and take the appropriate action.

Module 5: Coaching Others

Character: *Genuine Love*
Leaders respond in a patient, caring, and honest manner to those with whom they interact.

Competency: *Coaching Others*
Guide an individual through a thought process to discover insights and action steps that lead to further development in their life and leadership.

Module 6: Leading Meetings

Character: *Zeal*

Leaders demonstrate an enthusiastic commitment to that which God has called them to accomplish.

Competency: *Leading Meetings*

Plan and lead highly engaging meetings that enhance the team's productivity and unity.

Module 7: Review Your Progress

Self-evaluate to discover your strengths and your areas for growth.

1

Personal Development

As a rookie in ministry, I knew my leadership skills weren't up to par. It was just a matter of time until it became obvious to those around me. I was insecure and untrained. The people around me wanted to be led and were looking to me to help. I felt pressure to succeed and feared I'd be exposed as a failure.

That summer I signed up to attend my first John Maxwell leadership conference, hoping I'd find help. As I listened to him teach, I felt a longing to be a leader swell within me. Maxwell promoted a special offer on his leadership audiotapes, books, and devotionals by saying, "I guarantee if you buy this resource, and work your way through it over the next year, you will not be the same!" As I listened, I knew it wasn't a sales pitch; it was a leader who had the heart to see other leaders grow.

The problem was I didn't have the money to cover the $500 price tag. That evening I told my wife, Cindy, about the special deal, and her immediate response was, "You've got to get it."

I laughed, reminding her we didn't have $500. But she continued to persuade me. On the second day of the conference, I went back and sat through another round of leadership training and walked away, resisting the urge to make the purchase. But again, that evening,

Cindy urged me, saying, "Mac, if you're going to lead others, you have to first invest in yourself."

The next day I purchased the Personal Leadership Growth Kit. To this day, I consider it one of the best investments in my entire life. I listened to all one hundred tapes and read all the books within six months. As soon as I finished, I started relistening and rereading. Over the years, I wore those leadership tapes out. That one investment in my personal growth radically changed the trajectory of my life and leadership.

I've heard it said many times, "When you stop learning, you stop leading." Unfortunately, that's not entirely true. Many people continue to lead when they've stopped learning; they just don't lead well. Personal development is an essential discipline to healthy leadership in ministry.

You are going through this training because you are leading, or training to lead, a ministry department. Whether it is children's, student, worship, or outreach ministry, it's essential you continue to grow in the character and competencies that will help you effectively lead the entire tenure of your leadership.

When it comes to personal development, you can either grow accidentally or you can grow intentionally. But when you grow intentionally, it can change the trajectory of your life. You might think of it using this simple equation:

Time × Focus + Effort = Growth

For growth to happen, you'll need all three: time, focus, and effort. None of these are easy, but they are all vital to the development process. Many of you are likely good at applying these traits to various work projects. You are a leader, after all. What's difficult is that the work I'm suggesting here is personal. It's work on *you*.

I've discovered that sometimes the most difficult person to lead is myself. We have blind spots in our character or competencies that we can't see; we make excuses for our lack of growth; or sometimes, to be honest, we hit a season where we just aren't motivated to grow.

In this session, we are going to focus on the character trait of self-awareness and the competency of personal development, and explore how these work together to help you grow. Along the way, I will provide you with seven hacks to foster a life of growth so that you can create your own plan for personal development.

First, let's work to define our terms:

Character: *Self-Awareness*

Leaders are keenly aware and honest about how their emotional and behavioral tendencies impact those around them.

Competency: *Personal Development*

Continuously pursue learning opportunities to gain new insights and wisdom that enable growth in character and leadership competencies.

Objectives

1. Assess your level of self-awareness.
2. Evaluate the past thirty days of your personal development efforts.
3. Practice maximizing what you learn from reading this book.
4. Identify a personal development mentoring or accountability partner.
5. Create a thirty-day personal development plan using the template provided.

Deepen Your Character:
Self-Awareness

What is the most important trait for a leader? You might think it's integrity or a strong work ethic. Both are vital. However, without a high level of self-awareness, even the person with the highest level of integrity or work ethic will struggle to truly lead others. A recent study conducted by the Green Peak Partners and Cornell University found that a high self-awareness score was the strongest predictor of a leader's overall success.[1]

One of the greatest temptations for someone who leads a ministry department is to pretend to have all the answers. You know your team is looking to you, so you feel a pressure to be the expert in your area of ministry. But people tend to see through this type of pretense, and it can harm our credibility rather than help it.

When you lead with low self-awareness here's what happens:

- You find it difficult to influence others to actually follow you.
- You fail to grow in essential areas that help you improve as a leader and address your blind spots.
- You lose credibility with your team.
- You are unable to be fruitful and find fulfillment.
- You damage the culture of your organization through your attitudes or actions.

None of us come into leadership with perfect self-awareness, but we've likely been around certain leaders who really don't have it together in this area. The bully boss who intimidates her employees. The defensive leader who never takes the blame for anything. The controlling parents who micromanage their teenager. The victimized employee who always plays the martyr. These are but a few of the many examples of potential leaders who lack self-awareness and therefore struggle to lead anyone. Unfortunately, it's a lack of self-awareness that keeps these individuals from being cognizant of the negative impact their behavior is having on others, thus damaging their leadership credibility.

Scripture

Scripture provides a mirror by which we can all assess our self-awareness. As you read the following Scripture, meditate on what the author wishes to communicate, and answer the questions below. Allow the Holy Spirit to speak to you and challenge you as a leader so that you can grow in self-awareness in your everyday life.

Psalm 139:23–24

Search me, God, and know my heart;
test me and know my anxious thoughts.
See if there is any offensive way in me,
and lead me in the way everlasting.

God's word is clear that it is God who is able to search our hearts. We must invite him to test us, in order to help us see the ways our thoughts, motives, and actions might cause offense. For an effective leader, this must be a regular practice. We ask God to test us and reveal the things we need to see about ourselves.

Take a minute to read the entirety of Psalm 139 and answer the following questions:

In this psalm David reflects on four characteristics of God:

- Omniscient—he has perfect knowledge (1–6).
- Omnipresent—he is everywhere and is not limited by time or space (7–12).
- Omnipotent—he is all powerful (13–18).
- Holy—he is without sin, perfect in every way (19–24).

As David reflected on God's character, it led him to a moment of self-examination where he said, "Search me, God, and know my heart; test me and know my anxious thoughts. See if there is any offensive way in me, and lead me in the way everlasting" (23–24).

Which aspect of God's character in this psalm do you need to become more aware of? Why?

How would you assess your level of self-awareness: low, medium, or high? Explain the reasoning for your answer.

It is difficult to assess your level of self-awareness on your own. Who can you invite to give you feedback on your self-awareness?

If God were to point out an "offensive way" in your life right now, what do you think he would focus on?

What action steps can you take to grow in self-awareness?

Now that we have examined the character trait of self-awareness, we can begin to work through the core competency for this module: *Personal Development—continuously pursue learning opportunities to gain new insights and wisdom that enable growth in character and leadership competencies.* As you read what follows, note how self-awareness can undergird a leader's competency of personal development.

Develop Your Competency:
Personal Development
Preassessment

Before proceeding, complete the assessment below. In the final module of this training guide, you will retake it as a postassessment to measure your transformation and growth in this competency.

The following proficiencies demonstrate mastery of this module's competency. For each of them, give yourself a grade of A, B, C, D or E to reflect your actual level of competency today. Giving yourself an A+ indicates you are a model for others to follow. An E indicates no mastery.

Proficiency	Preassessment
I can easily articulate areas of growth God desires in my character or competency.	
I can demonstrate a high degree of intentionality with personal development plans.	
I use a system to maximize learning retention.	
I regularly learn from high-capacity leaders.	
I leverage the benefits of accountability for personal development.	

Reflection Questions

What barriers to consistent personal development do you most commonly face?

Pick one barrier and write below three ways you can eliminate that barrier.

What do you hope to gain from this session?

Growing on Purpose

I was in trouble but didn't know it. We'd recently planted a church, and my pace of life was out of bounds. A friend invited me to attend a one-day workshop for pastors in our city. I took the time to go because the speaker was a nationally known pastor who was one of my ministry heroes.

I was not disappointed. The substance of the talk and the spirit of the man rocked me! At the end of the workshop, my friend noticed how I had been impacted by the day. "Mac, I'm glad you had a good day," he said. "One of the things I've always admired about you is your constant pursuit of personal growth. But if I'm honest, as I've watched you over the past three years, I've seen your soul become emaciated."

Ouch!

"Emaciated." Thin. Weak.

That word hit me hard, and I knew I could never allow my soul to get in that condition again.

As a ministry leader, the temptation is to give of yourself over and over—to feed and care for the souls of those God has entrusted to you. This is good and right. But if you are not careful, you get so busy feeding and growing others, you forget to feed and develop yourself. How do you avoid that fate? Let me suggest seven growth hacks that will keep you engaged in developing your character and competency as a leader. I am not talking about your personal devotional time. While that is undoubtedly important, the focus here is on personal development in your leadership. Consider Jesus: Even the Son of God grew in wisdom and stature as he began his ministry.[2] If I want to be like Jesus then I need to grow in wisdom as well. That means a commitment to continual development.

Hack #1: Think About Personal Development As a Spiritual Discipline

While you may learn from many others, God is your primary personal development coach. And when he coaches you, his objective is to help you learn to live and lead like Jesus. Remember the bold prayer David prays in Psalm 139, "Search me … test me … see if there is any offensive way in me."

David was inviting God to examine him. The Hebrew word for "search" is a military term used for scouting out enemy territory. This is no causal request; David was calling for God to do a full-scale investigation of his heart.

David never pretended to be an innocent man; he knew full well that his past was riddled with sin. Yet, despite his sin-stained heart, David urged God to take a close look at his innermost thoughts. This process— though sometimes motivated by the consequences of our sin—should be an intentional discipline we pursue, in the same way we pursue other spiritual disciplines, such as Bible reading, prayer, and fasting. Talking to God about our growth as leaders should lead to greater self-awareness.

Growth requires truth. The easiest person to lie to is yourself. When you lie to yourself, you hurt yourself and others as well. Being honest about your leadership deficiencies requires humility and courage. While it may be difficult, the payoff is significant.

Self-awareness is the ability to be honest with yourself about yourself. It's having insight into your emotional and behavioral tendencies and how they affect those around you. Understanding why you behave the way you do and what needs to change is a sign you are growing in self-awareness.

Hack #2: Focus Your Efforts

Self-awareness requires giving yourself to an intentional process that is personal in nature. God has made you uniquely *you*—and only you can work on your life. If you want to grow in knowing who you are—and to learn to become the best version of you—it will require a focused effort.

There are two types of focus when it comes to personal growth: *dispersed focus* (unintentional) and *deliberate focus* (intentional). Dispersed focus was my default orientation for years. In any given month, I would be reading a few books, listening to a variety of podcasts, surfing random blog articles, and attending as many online webinars as I could. Many of these were in areas that were helping me grow as a leader, but they were not intentional. I'd invest hours in preaching, spiritual disciplines, personal finances, productivity, and many other topics. But I did not have a plan. So before long I'd spent countless hours reading and listening to useful content but was not able to retain or apply much along the way. When our focus is dispersed focus, we spread our development efforts among multiple learning focus points.

It might look something like this:

March 2020

Resource	Topic	Time
Book	Spiritual disciplines	3 hours
Podcast	Health	1 hour
Podcast	Personal finance	30 mins
Podcast	Starting a business	2 hours
YouTube	Sermon on prayer	30 mins
YouTube	Motivating teams	2 hours
Webinar	Leading in crisis	1 hour
Articles/Blogs	Building systems	2 hours
	Total: 8 topics	**Total: 12 hours**

In this example you notice this individual spent twelve hours attempting to grow in eight different topics.

There are three problems with this approach. First, dispersed focus actually works against how your brain is designed to function. Second, it limits your ability to remember what you've learned. And, finally, it slows down your overall rate of growth.

Deliberate focus, on the other hand, is a much more robust approach to personal growth. Deliberate focus aligns development efforts toward one objective or theme.

In my previous example, there were twelve hours of personal growth time. Let's look at what can happen with those same twelve hours when we adopt a more deliberate focus. It's important to first choose an area in which you want to grow. It could be an area of character or competency. For example, if I were to choose the area of empowering leaders then I would attempt to read books and blogs and listen to podcasts that focus on that singular theme before moving on to something else. To increase your personal development, choose one area to focus on at a time, and pour a disproportionate amount of time and energy into that area.

April 2020

Resource	Topic	Time
Book	Parenting teens	3 hours
Podcast	Health	1 hour
Podcast .	Personal finance	30 mins
Podcast	Parenting teens	2 hours
YouTube	Sermon on parenting	30 mins
YouTube	Parenting teens	2 hours
Webinar	Leading in crisis	1 hour
Articles/Blogs	Parenting teens	2 hours
	Total: 4 topics	**Total: 12 hours**

In this example the individual spent twelve hours attempting to grow but focused primarily (nine hours, thirty minutes) on the topic of parenting teens.

Fill in the chart below to evaluate your personal development efforts from the past thirty days:

Resources	Topics	Time	Takeaways

How would you evaluate the intentionality of your development time on a scale of 1–5: 1 – I am not intentional, 3 – I am somewhat intentional, 5 – I am highly intentional?

What would you change to make that development time more deliberate?

Hack #3: Write Out a Specific Plan

The more specific you are with your development plan, the more significant the growth you will experience. A written plan is not that difficult. Here are three steps you can take to build a written growth plan.

- **Identify the area in which you want to grow**

I would suggest you focus on either a character trait or a competency. You can use a simple chart to make a list of the traits and competencies that we discuss in this book. Then pick one area and begin. It's wise to start by focusing on growing your strengths rather than attempting to bring change to your most apparent weakness. Your strengths are areas where you are uniquely gifted and passionate, so it will be easier for you to start here. Then you can move on to the more difficult areas over time. Below is an example chart.

Character	Competencies /Leadership Skills
Discipline	Preaching
Honesty	Helping others
Humility	People skills
Generosity	Decision making
Love	Delegation
Integrity	Equipping
Patience	Saying no
Discernment	Multiplying
Sacrifice	Money management

What would you add to each list in the table above?

What one growth area would you like to start with first?

- **Choose a time frame**

When I first started the discipline of writing growth plans, I created them on an annual basis. Guess what? I never completed one. Typically, I would write out three or four areas in which I wanted to grow, along with a plan for growing in those areas. But a lot can change in twelve months, and it's hard to maintain focus over that length of time. I'd suggest that you focus on something you can do in thirty to sixty days.

- **Put it in writing**

Many people know where they want to grow but are unsure how to turn that into a plan. Writing down the plan is simple. After you've identified your growth statement, take twenty to thirty minutes, a blank piece of paper, and answer these five questions.

   o   What will I read?

- What will I watch or listen to?
- Who can I talk to?
- Who can I watch?
- How can I practice?

The answers to those questions become your plan. So it might look like this:

Growth area: Increase my ability to focus.
Time frame: 30 Days
- What will I read?
  - *The One Thing* by Gary Keller and Jay Papasan
  - *Atomic Habits* by James Clear
- What will I watch or listen to?
  - YouTube—"5 Ways to Build Focus," Thomas Frank
  - YouTube—"Master Your Focus," Cal Newport
  - YouTube—"Essentialism," Google Talks, Greg McKeown
- Who can I talk to?
  - Mike G
  - Tim P
- Who can I watch?
  - Colleen F
- How can I practice?
  - Time block my weekdays
  - Put tasks on my calendar
  - Use the Pomodoro method daily
  - Evaluate my focus each day by giving myself an A–F grade

You can also go to multiplygroup.org/tcfreesample to download a sample of one of our Competency Training Cards. The Training Card workbook has thirty-two different competencies along with growth plan suggestions.

Hack #4: Stop Reading Books

This is not the counsel you might expect from an author, but hear me out. In my early twenties I became a passionate reader. I struggled to lead well, so the best option I knew was to read as many leadership books as possible.

Don't get me wrong. Those books were helpful to a point. But much of my reading time just ended up being wasted time.

A typical book takes about four to six hours to read. So in my early days, I would read a book to learn. My goal was to read it as fast as I could. Then I would move on to the next book.

A few years into that routine, I realized I wasn't benefiting as much as I had hoped. Then it hit me. I need to stop *reading* books and start *studying* books. The same applies to watching videos or listening to audios. Here are a few tips on how to study a book to help you retain more of what you're learning.[3]

- **Get the big picture**

A quick scan of the table of contents of many books is beneficial. The author has organized the book logically and intentionally. So reading through the table of contents can give you a sequence and a breakdown of the topics covered, and it can give your brain the big picture it desires.

- **Take strategic notes**

I always read on my iPad Kindle app. That way, I can highlight things that stand out to me and capture them later to put in my Evernote file. But I also read with a notebook beside me. I don't write much in it, but what I do write is strategic.

When I read a book, I want to capture five to seven *big* takeaways. These are the significant lessons that stood out to me from the book. As I read each chapter, if something of great prominence strikes me, I write down the concept. I try to be selective here, so that I'm only noting really critical concepts.

I also grab good story illustrations. When I was thirty years old, I heard John Maxwell describe how one of his daily disciplines is filing. As he reads or hears a good story, he writes down the theme and files it away to use it in his speaking or writing. As a young communicator, I was so impressed, I adopted that same discipline.

Finally, I try to note action steps. This is probably the most important discipline. Reading stimulates your thinking, and during a one-hour reading session, I probably think to myself ten times, "I need to ..." So I draw an arrow and write down the action I want to take. Later on, I transfer those arrows to my digital task management system.

■ Teach what you learn

Are you ready to take learning to the next level? Teach what you learn.

This past year I decided to learn cartooning. After several hours of reading books and watching videos, I could tell my skill was growing. So one weekend, I gathered my four grandchildren and taught them how to use basic shapes for drawing a cartoon. It was amazing how teaching them challenged me to recall and articulate what I was learning. Teaching is one of the best ways to reinforce helpful content.

Which of the tips above is most helpful to you? Why?

How will you apply this section this week?

Hack #5: Practice, Practice, Practice

My friends laughed when, at age fifty-seven, I decided to take up boxing.

I didn't do it because I am a Mike Tyson wannabe or because I'm fearful I will get in a fistfight. I am continually training others to teach, so I thought it would be a good idea to learn something that I had never done and was, frankly, something I didn't know much about.

As I walked into my first session, I thought to myself: *How hard can boxing be, right?* Well, much to my surprise, the answer is, *Really hard!* It takes much more coordination than I ever imagined.

My trainer, who was barely out of high school, reminded me of the importance of practice with a simple drill. Every time I would throw a jab, I would hold my arm incorrectly. After telling me a hundred times I was doing it wrong, he put the left side of my body against the wall. He tucked a magazine under my right arm and told me to start throwing jabs and to not stop for three minutes. I thought this kid had finally lost it with me. But ninety seconds into the exercise, I dropped the magazine and yelled out, "I got it!" Everything he had been telling me and showing me finally clicked in my brain because I'd been forced to do it the right way over and over again.

Whenever you are learning a new skill, your brain has to rewire the way it thinks. The neurons in your brain work to connect with other neurons to create new neurological pathways. When they first connect, the new connections travel at around 2 mph. But with practice, the new communication pathway (skill) gets faster and faster until they reach speeds of up to 270 mph.[4]

Imagine I read two books and watch a video series on how to box. But I never put on the gloves or get near a heavy bag. I'm gaining a lot of information, but the lack of practice prevents me from developing the perfect left jab-cross combination.

This is the way many people read a book. They read books on leadership, but they never put anything into practice. So as you read, identify ways you can practice the thing you want to learn.

For example, my January growth plan was to grow in focus. As part of my growth plan, I read *Atomic Habits* by James Clear. Here are a few things I wrote down to help me grow in remaining focused:

- Use the Pomodoro Technique.[5]

- Put tasks on the calendar, not just my to-do list.
- Create an environment for writing.
- Develop a routine for writing and drawing cartoons.

I needed to practice these disciplines for this level of focus to become habitual for me. And so do you.

Hack #6: Get Around "Big" People

If you want to grow as a leader, one of the best things you can do is get around a "big" leader. A big leader is someone whose character you admire. It's not just someone who appears "successful." It's someone who has bigger faith, wisdom, character, vision, competency, or experience than you.

When I was twenty-seven years old, I had the opportunity to work for a pastor in Dallas, Texas who I would call a big leader. He was in his mid-forties, and he'd already accomplished what most people would have been happy to achieve in a lifetime. And he had big influence, big vision, and big character. And most of all, he had a big impact on my life. To this day, I point to my two years with him as the most significant growth experience in my life.

In chapter 12 of Hebrews, the author gives insight into how to get around big people. "Therefore, since we are surrounded by such a great cloud of witnesses [big people], let us throw off everything that hinders and the sin that so easily entangles. And let us run with perseverance the race marked out for us" (Hebrews 12:1–2). Here are three crucial lessons from this passage.

- **Big leaders are a model for us to follow**

God wants me to look at the life and faith of other great leaders. It sometimes seems hard to find a hero to model yourself after in today's culture. But here, the author of Hebrews reminds us that we're surrounded by great people, if we just look around.

The Greek word for "surrounded" conveys the idea of a high wall that completely encircles you. In other words, it's difficult to miss. But sometimes, we still miss seeing the obvious. But don't miss the obvious big leaders you have easy access to. In today's world, it's fairly easy to position your life to get around big leaders, even if your exposure to them is initially limited to their books, podcasts, or webinars.

Obviously, the best scenario is to learn from someone in person. If you don't know the person you want to learn from, don't let that stop you. Take a risk, especially if you are a young leader. Email the individual you admire and let them know that you'd like to learn from them and ask for a thirty-minute meeting or phone call. Don't fail to capitalize on this growth approach just because you don't know someone personally.

■ Big leaders inspire us to make big changes

The passage goes on to say, "Let us throw off everything that hinders." As we go through life, it's easy to pick up some bad habits, wrong attitudes, or sinful patterns that can hold us back from maximizing our leadership effectiveness. This is why we must get around godly leaders. Every time I'm around a big leader, I see changes I need to make in my own life when I compare my own growth and development to theirs.

Left to our own devices, we tend to follow our emotions or assumptions when determining our next growth step. But if big leaders are able to speak into our lives, they generally guide us in a direction we might not have chosen on our own. As a result, we can grow in areas that will accelerate our leadership.

- **Big leaders show us how to finish strong**

The lives and examples of big leaders can motivate us to keep the course when leadership gets tough, which it inevitably will. There are times when we want to quit, right? But when we look at those we admire and see the struggles they've been through and how they handled these challenges, we are inspired to finish strong.

A few years ago, Cindy and I had the opportunity to go on an overseas missions trip with an influential megachurch leader. This leader had recently experienced personal tragedy, but I was so impacted because he spoke openly and honestly about his feelings. His pain was evident, but so was his passion and perseverance. As I listened to him share what he went through, it made my problems and struggles pale in comparison, and it taught me a great deal about how to work through hard things as a leader. This pastor served as a great example of how to persevere and trust God to help us finish strong, regardless of what might happen in our lives.

I've learned it's essential for me to get around big leaders. It gives me a clear picture of the whys and hows required to lead at a higher level. And this has proven to be one of the most productive growth disciplines in my life.

List the names of three big leaders you would like to learn from.

What are three questions you would ask if you had the opportunity to meet one of them?

Hack #7: Embrace Mentoring and Accountability

My heart raced with excitement when I realized I had the opportunity to sit one-on-one with Matt Chandler and study through Philippians. I could envision it in my mind—sitting in Starbucks, pen ready, Bible open, drinking a venti cold brew and a big cup of Matt's wisdom.

Now, I have to be honest with you, this was not a formal in-person mentoring relationship. It was an eight-week video course I stumbled upon when I was doing one of those mindless Google searches. Yet I had struck gold and was motivated to seize the learning opportunity. Grabbing my trusty moleskin journal from my bookbag, I consumed session one.

The next day I was a little too busy to do session two. Another day passed, and another without logging into the course. Before I knew it, two weeks were gone, and so was my motivation. There's no doubt your motivation for personal development will be affected by distractions. Distractions lead to delays. Delays lead to the death of motivation.

Consistency with personal growth requires accountability, even when we have a chance to develop under the care of the biggest leaders of our day.

The American Society of Training and Development (ASTD) found the following in a recent study:

- 65% of their participants completed a goal if they asked someone to hold them accountable to their goals *and* fully committed to accomplishing their project with their accountability partner.
- 95% of people successfully met their goals when they did the above *and* attended a specific appointment with their accountability partner to discuss their progress and success.[6]

The point is obvious—if you want to grow in character or competency then you need a plan and a partner. You have to get serious about accountability. I define accountability as *partnering with an individual to provide consistent encouragement and challenge to achieve an objective that is essential to personal development.*

This definition should lead you to four questions:

i.   Do I have a specific area of character or competency God wants me to grow in?
ii. Who would be willing to partner with me in my development?
iii. Can that person provide both encouragement *and* challenge?
iv. Will we both commit to being consistent in our form of accountability, whether it be a meeting, phone call, or text?

Don't let further delays hold you back from growing into the leader God has called you to be. The process is simple. Find a person and ask them to help you. Then shadow them for a day and take notes on what you observe from their life and leadership. Next, share with them the personal growth plan you developed and the characteristic or competency you are focusing on at that time. If you are working with a mentor who excels in a specific area or department, you might ask them to help you build a list of competencies that are necessary in that area of ministry. From there, you can begin to build a resource library of books, blogs, podcasts, and other tools you can study to grow in these defined areas.

We grow better when we have other people speaking into our lives. We grow faster when we have a leadership coach or a peer holding us accountable. We will experience a depth of transformation when we submit ourselves to the influence of a godly mentor or peer who can speak truth into our lives.

Young leaders, who are you going to ask to pour into you over the next year?

Seasoned leaders, what are you going to do this year to push yourself to another level?

Conclusion

Here's what I've discovered in over thirty years of leadership development: better leaders get better results. And better leaders take time for personal development, always learning and growing. This is why I never want to stop learning and growing. Time is too short, and the mission, too crucial.

Paul told his protégé Timothy, "This is a trustworthy saying: 'If someone aspires to be a church leader, he desires an honorable position'" (1 Timothy 3:1 NLT). That was true of me; Jesus had made such a difference in my life that I longed to lead and make a kingdom impact. My heart wanted a good thing, but I wasn't sure how to grow in my leadership.

In this chapter, I've attempted to provide you with a road map for that growth. Small, daily steps in the right direction go a long way over time. As you take steps, you'll grow in self-awareness and in turn become a leader who is committed to the work of personal development. And this work will not stop until we see Jesus face to face.

Put It Into Practice

Choose one or more of the following to complete prior to meeting with your trainer.

1. Create a list of character traits and competencies in which you would like to grow. Build on the list provided in this module. File your list somewhere you can access it readily when it's time to build a new growth plan.

2. Use the template provided in this module to build a thirty-day personal development plan. Identify an accountability partner who can help you stick with the plan. Or purchase the Personal Growth Plan Workbook to access thirty-two competency growth plans. You can find these at www.multiplygroup.org.

3. Reach out to a "big leader" and ask them for thirty to sixty minutes of their time, so you can ask them questions. Make a list of ten questions prior to meeting with them. Take a pen and notebook so you can record their answers. Share what you learned with your trainer.

4. Practice the advice from this module on reading books. Share with your trainer how this system of reading helped you retain and learn more.

5. Interview two to three people who lead the ministry department you lead or desire to lead. From these interviews create a list of five essential competencies for leading your specific ministry department. Share these with your trainer.

Reflect on Your Learning

Where did you grow the most in this competency?

What next step do you need to take to continue to grow in this competency?

Meet With Your Trainer

Consistent practice can be a great beginning to sharpening a skill, but developing a skill also requires processing what you learned with others. Meet with your trainer and discuss what you learned from this module.

Dig Deeper

If you are participating in an internship or want to continue to grow in the competency of personal development, go to www.maclakeonline.com/internshiptools to download the companion guide to this book.

---

[1] For more on this study see Victor Lipman, "All Successful Leaders Need This Quality: Self-Awareness," *Forbes*, November 18, 2013, www.forbes.com/sites/victorlipman/2013/11/18/all-successful-leaders-need-this-quality-self-awareness/#7944601a1f06.

[2] See Luke 2:52.

[3] For more, see my "How to Study a Book," YouTube, Jan 4, 2021, www.youtube.com/watch?v=0flxv4EVHpI&t=23s.

[4] See this article for more: Tim Welsh, "It Feels Instantaneous, but How Long Does It Really Take to Think a Thought?" *The Conversation*, June 26, 2015, https://theconversation.com/it-feels-instantaneous-but-how-long-does-it-really-take-to-think-a-thought-42392.

[5] Kat Boogaard, "Take It From Someone Who Hates Productivity Hacks— the Pomodoro Technique Actually Works," *The Muse*, https://www.themuse.com/advice/take-it-from-someone-who-hates-productivity-hacksthe-pomodoro-technique-actually-works.

[6] See Mui Tsun, "The Power of Accountability: How to Make Reaching Your Goals Almost a Certainty," August 20, 2020, https://www.muitsun.com/power-of-accountability/.

2

Time Management

I was a twenty-four-year-old struggling real estate agent whose bank account was quickly approaching single digits. So when a friend tried to convince me to invest a thousand dollars in stock, I was skeptical, to say the least. But he persisted. "Just invest for a year, and if you're patient, the return on that investment will be worth all the wait." Sure, I could have used that money over the course of the year, but I was promised a return on my investment, so I invested and waited.

One year later, I got the envelope in the mail. I tore it open, expecting a lucrative check, and what I found took my breath away: 648 dollars. I'd lost over 300 dollars from my original investment.

Not all investments bring a return, at least not all do in the stock market. However, our lives work a bit differently. We're given a set number of hours to invest each week—168 to be exact. Everyone gets the same amount. How we use those hours is up to us. Like the stock market, there are wise and unwise ways to invest. Unlike the stock market, however, the Bible provides us with greater clarity on what we should do with those hours to maximize our return on investment.

When you lead a ministry department you feel pulled in a million directions. There are people on your team you need to care for, events that need to be planned, guests that need following up, systems that need to be improved, leaders that need to be developed, and meetings or rehearsals you need to attend. Ministry runs like this fifty-two weeks a year. No wonder it's so easy for staff or high-capacity volunteers to get burned-out. Mismanagement of your time can erode your spiritual, mental, and physical health very quickly.

Paul writes, "Be very careful, then, how you live—not as unwise but as wise, making the most of every opportunity, because the days are evil" (Ephesians 5:15–16). The language of investing is helpful here. We don't *spend* our time, so much as we *invest* it. Time is a gift God deposits in your life every day. How you invest that time will determine the kingdom impact you have throughout your life. Bad investments get bad results.

In this module, you will discover the principles and techniques that will maximize your time investment.

First, let's work to define our terms:

Character: *Self-Discipline*
Leaders yield to the Holy Spirit, making the right decisions despite their emotions and temptations.

Competency: *Time Management*
Steward time in a wise manner that minimizes distractions and maximizes personal contribution to the organization's mission.

Objectives

1. Identify a specific area you need to grow in self-discipline.
2. Write a life mission statement.
3. Practice time blocking a week of tasks, events, and meetings.

4. Improve the quality of your times of solitude.

5. Identify your top three most common distractions.

Deepen Your Character: *Self-Discipline*

Being from the South, I am not a New England Patriots fan, but I do have an admiration for Tom Brady and what he has accomplished in his career with the Patriots and now the Tampa Bay Buccaneers. Brady is a seven-time Super Bowl champion and five-time winner of the Super Bowl Most Valuable Player Award. He has athletic talent, but talent only gets people so far. Brady has become well known for his "TB12 Method," a fitness and nutrition philosophy that enables him to achieve peak performance. Not only does his book of the same name explain his fitness program but it also reveals his exceptional self-discipline. Guys and girls like Brady don't become successful by chance. They discipline themselves for the work and, over time, their self-discipline produces astounding results.

The same is true for Christians. When you combine talent with self-discipline, the kingdom impact God can have through your life is unimaginable. We might be prone to think it's a lack of gifts that hinders the effectiveness of most Christians and Christian leaders. Not so much. Self-discipline, or a lack thereof, is a far greater contributing factor than gifting. The Apostle Paul tells us that everyone has a spiritual gift—a God-empowered ability. The Holy Spirit supernaturally empowers each of us in a specific area. The gifting comes from him, not from ourselves. So if God has given us gifts, we are positioned for the impact he wants us to make. But it is the lack of discipline, not the lack of gifting, that holds most people back.

A lack of self-discipline has stopped many ministry leaders from making more significant kingdom impact. Sexual impropriety, lack of financial integrity, misuse of time or power, and many other factors that overflow from a lack of self-discipline have put many leaders in the ditch and out of ministry.

Unfortunately, I've witnessed this firsthand too many times. I've known pastors who had a great passion for Jesus and his church. But over time, a lack of boundaries and discipline gave way to behaviors that eroded their character. And, as so many of us have witnessed, this can then be followed by a moral failure. Not only does the individual go through a personal crisis, but their behavior also impacts their immediate family, friends, and the church body at large. One staff member who morally falls can cause a domino effect that eats away at the faith of others around them. All of this can be redeemed, but the initial impact is devastating to so many.

As leaders of a ministry department, we must remember:

- The way you lead your area of ministry should come from an overflow of your walk with Jesus.
- You're not just called to do ministry; you're called to model a Christlike life.
- Choosing not to overextend yourself and to create healthy boundaries can help those on your team establish healthy boundaries in their own life.

Self-discipline can protect you from a spiritual moral crash and guard you against simple things that ruin your leadership credibility. A primary foundation of self-discipline is a solid investment of your time. Your ability to bring yourself under control with the help of the

Holy Spirit and do what you need to do each day makes a difference. Being disciplined in how you manage your time will enable you to complete important tasks and responsibilities and gain the respect of others on your team.

Harry Truman once said, "In reading the lives of great men, I found that the first victory they won was over themselves. Self-discipline with all of them came first." If we fail to develop self-control, there is a risk to our physical health, our relationships, and our spiritual health. It can rob us of the potential God has for us in our lives and limit the investment we can make with the time we are given.

Scripture

As you read the following Scripture, meditate on what the author wishes to communicate, and answer the questions below. Allow the Holy Spirit to speak to you and challenge you as a leader on how you can develop your character so that you are self-disciplined in your everyday life.

1 Corinthians 9:24–27

Do you not know that in a race all the runners run, but only one gets the prize? Run in such a way as to get the prize. Everyone who competes in the games goes into strict training. They do it to get a crown that will not last, but we do it to get a crown that will last forever. Therefore I do not run like someone running aimlessly; I do not fight like a boxer beating the air. No, I strike a blow to my body and make it my slave so that after I have preached to others, I myself will not be disqualified for the prize.

Paul says he runs in a way to get the prize. He disciplines himself so he will not be disqualified from the prize. What do you think the "prize" was for Paul? What is the prize for you? (Be as specific as possible.)

What does "strict training" look like in your life?

Think of an area in which you need to be more self-disciplined? Why do you struggle in this particular area? In what way does or could this area of struggle hurt your credibility as a leader of a ministry? What are two or three things you can do this week to demonstrate more self-discipline in this area?

Now that we have examined the character trait of self-discipline, we can begin to work through the core competency for this module: *Time Management—steward time in a wise manner that minimizes distractions and maximizes personal contribution to the organization's mission.* As you read what follows, note how self-discipline can undergird a leader's competency of time management.

Develop Your Competency:
Time Management
Preassessment

Before proceeding, complete the assessment below. In the final module of this training guide, you will retake it as a postassessment to measure your transformation and growth in this competency.

The following proficiencies demonstrate mastery of this module's competency. For each of them, give yourself a grade of A, B, C, D, or E to reflect your actual level of competency today. Giving yourself an A+ indicates you are a model for others to follow. An E indicates no mastery.

Proficiency	Preassessment
I make decisions on how to use time, based on personal strengths and mission.	
I consistently prioritize assignments from most important to least important.	
I routinely block out how time will be used on the calendar.	
I say "no" to non-essential tasks or opportunities that do not align with priorities.	
I intentionally block out distractions in order to stay focused on priority assignments.	

Reflection Questions

Which of the proficiencies above reflect your top time-management strength?

Which one reflects your top time-management growth area?

What do you hope to gain from this session?

Making Wise Time Investments

Why is time so difficult to manage? Time is constant. One minute is always sixty seconds. One hour is always sixty minutes. And one day is consistently twenty-four hours. You would think this level of consistency would enable us to master how we invest time. But while time is constant, the way we use time is not. When leading a ministry, we have so much flying at us on any given day. Some of it is self-imposed chaos and some the result of living in a chaotic world. It's difficult to know how we should invest our time and even more difficult to actually do what we know we should.

In my first full-time ministry position, I overestimated what I could get done in a week, continually missed deadlines, and lived a hurried life. I recognized my need to grow in my ability to manage time. So, I purchased Stephen Covey's book *First Things First*. He told a story that had a profound impact on the way I viewed my schedule.

Covey shared how an instructor at a seminar set a wide-mouth gallon jar on a table. The instructor then put as many fist-sized rocks into the jar as he could. Then he asked the students if the jar was full. They agreed that it was. He then took gravel and poured it into the jar, shaking it so that pieces of stone slid into spaces between the big rocks. Again, he asked the students if the jar was full. They agreed it was. Next, he poured in the sand. And when no more sand could fit, he poured water into the jar. Only then was the jar full. As the instructor pointed out to the students, if he'd started out filling the jar with sand and gravel, he never would have been able to fit in all the big rocks.[1]

The point of the story is not that you can squeeze more into a day than you think. The point is to make sure you put the big rocks in your schedule first. Focus on getting the most important things done, and you will be less stressed and more productive.

That was it! I was putting small things into my schedule first. Small stones are more comfortable to pick up. They tend to be more fun or have a greater sense of urgency. The problem is that the small stones rarely move the needle in those areas that are key priorities. While some small stones can make us feel like we are making progress, they are rarely those things that help us move toward the most important aspects of our mission.

The big rocks are essential. They are the tasks and conversations that actually make things happen. They are what we need to focus on because they are the most strategic endeavors we can undertake with our 168 hours.

But the gaps between the stones are also important. It's in this space that we leave room for rest, celebration, and imaginative thinking.

Seven Tips for Wise Investment of Time

After over thirty years of ministry, I can tell you, most of the stress we feel from ministry is self-induced. We try to do too much, too quickly, and squeeze as much as possible into our calendar. Here are seven ways I've grown in making wise time investments.

Tip #1: Stay on Mission

The way we use our time doesn't always demonstrate the importance of the mission God has given us. The primary filter for how we invest our time should be God's mission for our lives. Does the activity I am choosing serve to advance the mission or not?

Years ago, God made clear that the mission of my life boiled down to two words: *multiplying multipliers*. If I use my time doing tasks that don't contribute to that mission, I am a poor steward of God's calling on my life. When I use my time multiplying multipliers then

I've invested in ways that both honor God and advance his mission in the world, often in ways that astound me.

Staying on mission can be a challenge for many people in ministry. The strong pull to love and serve people can create an emotional tension, especially when we see so much need around us. In our frenzied activity, we often miss the very best things God is asking us, uniquely, to do. I am convinced that many people in ministry are overly stressed because they are doing activities God has not asked them to do.

This is why I tell young leaders that time management is not just a logical activity. It is an emotional and spiritual activity. Planning your day is a very straightforward and logical task. But, during the day, the pull to please others can take you away from the thing God has called you to do. Saying "no" is an emotional decision because it forces us to go back to our mission. We can't let people-pleasing or selfish pursuits derail us from God's best. Jesus didn't allow the emotional pull of people-pleasing determine how he invested his time. If it was okay for Jesus to say "no" to people, I think we are safe to do so as well.

Mark 1 is a unique snapshot of Jesus' life because Mark gives us a glimpse into how Jesus invested twenty-four hours. In the morning, Jesus and his disciples went to the synagogue where he taught. Next, they went to Peter's mother-in-law's house where undoubtedly they had a meal. But Peter's mother-in-law was sick, so Jesus healed her. Late that afternoon, crowds showed up at the house, and Jesus spent the evening healing many people. The next day Jesus got up early to pray. Crowds showed up early that morning looking for Jesus to heal and teach. When the disciples found him and demanded he come back to the masses, Jesus said "no." He continued, "Let us go somewhere else—to the nearby villages—so I can preach there also. That is why I have come" (Mark 1:38).

Jesus based his decision on the mission the Father had given him, not the needs of the people around him. And it's the same basis for decision making that you and I should have as well.

Lou Holtz, the famous Notre Dame football coach, taught his players to use the acronym WIN. It stands for *What's Important Now?* Holtz would remind his players to ask themselves this question over and over throughout the day as a way of forcing themselves to constantly assess if they were staying true to their mission.

Each morning I end my time with God with the same question: *What are the three most essential WINs for today?* I write those in my journal, and at the end of the day, I mark off each one with green (completed), yellow (partially completed), or red (not completed). The process of beginning my day with my unique mission and then evaluating my day against that mission has made me a better leader.

How would you describe your life mission in one sentence?

How well did you align your activities from last week with that mission? Put three answers under each column on the next page.

Things I did that were on mission	Things I did that were not on mission

Tip #2: Prioritize the Right Things

Do you ever question the sacrifices you make for the gospel? Jesus calls us to a life of sacrifice. In Luke 9:23 he said, "Whoever wants to be my disciple must deny themselves and take up their cross daily and follow me." Over the years, I've watched dedicated Christ-followers do this very thing by giving up prestige, power, lucrative careers, comfort, and even personal dreams to follow Christ into full-time vocational ministry. Choosing a life of sacrifice, they dedicate 100 percent of their lives for kingdom causes.

Sometimes leaders mistakenly confuse busyness, harried activity or workaholism as sacrifice. Like Christ, Paul urges a life of sacrifice.

In Romans 12, he challenges us to present our bodies as a living sacrifice. But look at the result, "Then you will be able to test and approve what God's will is—his good, pleasing and perfect will" (Romans 12: 2). I don't think God's will is for our physical, emotional, or relational health to deteriorate. There are some things God never asks us to sacrifice. Below are some tips to ensure we don't neglect the important things in life.

Look after yourself physically. Too many pastors run on crazy schedules, failing to take care of themselves physically and totally ignoring the disciplines of exercise and healthy eating. In 1 Corinthians 6:19–20, Paul tells us our bodies are the temple of the Holy Spirit. Yet oftentimes we consider the mismanagement of our health to be a lesser sin. Anyone who says, "I'm too busy to exercise" is in danger of reducing the efficiency and effectiveness of future ministry.

Protect your marriage. God also doesn't ask us to sacrifice our marriage. I was recently talking with a friend about pastors who have moral failures in their marriage, and he shared something incredibly insightful: "A man who has an affair with ministry makes himself more vulnerable to an affair with another woman." God designed the husband-wife relationship to complete one another (Genesis 2:18). Yet many couples find that the demands of ministry actually drive them further apart. God never asked us to sacrifice our marriage for the sake of the gospel. We can easily begin to view our marriage partner solely as a ministry partner, and when we do, we begin to use them, instead of love and serve them.

Involve your family. Many pastors, especially church planters, have children who are in the formative years of life. Right after Cindy and I announced we were going to plant a church back in 1997, I heard a well-known pastor exclaim, "If you have young children, *do not* plant a church!" That terrified us, but it was too late—the journey had begun, and the calling was too obvious. So right then and there, we decided that our kids would be better because of ministry. To be honest it was difficult. The demands of planting were high. But we worked hard to have special times with our kids, show them the benefits of being in ministry, and include them in the God-moments along our ministry journey. Ministry can be a great classroom in which our children have a front-row seat to witness the provision and power of God. But ministry can also be a preoccupation that causes us to put parenting on autopilot.

I'll never forget driving down the road when my kids were younger, and one of my sons said, "Dad I hate you being a pastor." When I asked why, he spoke of my constant distraction with serving "my church." While I never would have said it out loud, my behavior screamed that "God needs me in order to accomplish his work in my community." That's pride. That's a low view of God. And that's an attitude that leads pastors down a dangerous path. A preoccupation with ministry communicates to our children that our relationship with "our church" is a greater priority than our relationship with them.

Pursue silence and solitude. In order to avoid sacrificing the wrong things, we must be the kind of leaders who pursue silence and solitude to help us keep our priorities in order. Jesus did this. He got away to prepare for a major task (Luke 4:1–2, 14–15), to recharge after hard work (Mark 6:30–32), to work through grief (Matthew 14:1–13), before making an important decision (Luke 6:12–13), in times of distress (Luke 22:39–44), and to focus on prayer (Luke 5:16).[2] As a leader, we can be certain that we need the same time of solitude because we are going to be faced with similar difficulties. If we don't have healthy pressure releases, then we will cut corners in areas we shouldn't sacrifice and miss the best of God's mission for our lives.

Which of the areas below are you doing best with?

- Taking care of myself physically
- Protecting my marriage
- Involving my family
- Pursuing silence and solitude

Which do you need to do better?

What practical step can you take over the next thirty days to do better in the area you need to improve?

How often have you intentionally scheduled solitude into your calendar over the past thirty days?

Think back to your last day off. Were you able to completely disconnect, or were you still preoccupied with work? If you were preoccupied with work, why?

What do you need to implement in order to protect yourself from working too much?

Tip #3: Know Yourself

If you want to be a master at time management, you must have a masterful understanding of yourself. God created you with specific passions, gifts, and strengths. When you operate in those, you are functioning as God intended. This means that everyone is designed to use the 168 hours of their week in different ways and that some people can do certain work in one of those hours that might take another person ten hours to accomplish at the same level of proficiency.

It's easy to waste way too much time doing things we are not good at. In my first full-time ministry position at Pawleys Island Baptist Church, I tried to do what I was good at, but I also tried to do all the things I wasn't good at. For example, I am good at creating leadership training sessions. I could sit in a coffee shop and knock one out in thirty to forty-five minutes. But I am not good at writing interesting articles. So when it came time to write the monthly newsletter, instead of finding someone who was good at writing, you guessed it, I'd do it myself. Writing a five-hundred-word article would take a good writer about thirty to forty-five minutes. But I would labor for hours, even a full day, to hammer out a short, poorly written newsletter. That was not a good use of my time or talent.

Some people say time flies when you're having fun. It's more apt to say time flies when we are doing things we love and are skilled in. There are three key questions you need to ask yourself to invest time wisely:

- What do I do best?
- What brings me the most energy?
- When am I at my best?

Now, the key in life is to get yourself in a position where your job lines up with who you are, meaning that you should make it your ambition to find work that allows you to do the kinds of things that correspond with your answers to the previous three questions. You'll likely never be able to *only* do these things, but you should be able to find a role where you can do these things for the majority of the time.

At least twice a year I ask my staff this question: What percentage of your time are you operating in your strengths? If they answer anything below 80 percent, I follow up by asking them what I can do to help get them back up to the 80 percent zone. People need to operate in their areas of strength because if they don't, they will lose their joy in the role or not bring their best to the work. When you invest time doing something you love, it increases your energy level. If you invest time doing things you don't enjoy or are not good at, it decreases your energy level. You likely know that to be true in your own life.

In Marcus Buckingham's book, *Go Put Your Strengths to Work*, he recommends carrying a set of green cards and red cards for one week. Each time you do a task or activity that brings you energy, write down what it was on the green card. Each time you do a task that you do not enjoy and drains your energy, write it down on the red card. At the end of the week, you put the cards in two stacks. Study the items on the red cards and summarize these as your weaknesses. Next, study the items on the green cards and summarize these into your top three to five strengths.[3]

The application is obvious. Plan your days doing as many things as possible that fit onto the green cards. The aim is to do what God is asking you to do. More is not always better. That is a tough pill to swallow for high achievers or those who love to check off boxes on their task list. If you focus on more, you may miss the mission. The goal is not more; the goal is the mission God has given you.

What three words describe your strengths?

If you were to write a job description for yourself, what would it include?

What are your top three responsibilities?

What are you good at, and does it align with what you are responsible for? If the answer is "no," what do you need to change?

Tip #4: Leverage the Strengths of Your Team

Most of us approach time management from a personal perspective—I am responsible for managing my time; you are responsible for managing yours. But time management is more like a team sport. In the previous section, I stressed the importance of knowing your strengths. But as a leader, you must know the strengths of your team as well.

The whole purpose of a team is to assign specific roles to individuals who have strengths in particular areas. When you know your team's strengths, you can work together to make sure everyone is not only maximizing their talents but maximizing their time as well.

You are also far more likely to give away responsibility when you know that someone else is more gifted, competent, and passionate about an area than you are. There's a tendency to fill your time with tasks because, well, "someone's gotta do it." But when it's not just any old "someone" who has to do it but it's a person who is uniquely designed to give care and attention to the work, then you, as a leader, should find freedom and joy in letting them run after the things that they are uniquely built to do. You can say "no" because it's an act of empowerment for someone else on your team.

This flows from the rock principle that we learned earlier. A big rock for you as a leader might be doing the hard work of getting to know your team. You might be tempted to tackle all of the little rocks of each project, but by getting to know the gifts of others on your team, you are better able to empower them to make good use of their 168 hours.

Tip #5: Plan Your Time

You waste more time than you think. If I waste money, I might be able to work hard and earn more to replace it. But wasted time cannot be replaced. It's just gone.

At age twenty-nine, as the associate pastor at Pawleys Island Baptist Church, I had more ideas than I had time. As a result, I was hurried, unfocused, and always stressed. A seasoned leader recommended I did a deep dive study into Peter Drucker's book, *The Effective Executive*. Chapter two of that book rocked my world. It's titled, "Know Thy Time." In that chapter, Drucker challenges the reader to track time in fifteen-minute increments for a full week.[4]

So I printed the one-week calendar and put it into practice. (Remember from the last chapter—you want to study and apply what you learn from books, not just read them.) At the end of the week, I was shocked at how much time I had wasted. Small distractions were leading to diminished production for the time I was investing. That was when I learned the concept of time blocking.

Time blocking is a time management method where you block your day into sixty- to ninety-minute segments. Each block is dedicated to accomplishing something specific.

For example, today, I have eight time-blocks planned for my day.

- Block 1: 8:30–10 a.m. – write a chapter of a new book
- Block 2: 10:15–11:30 a.m. – emails, calls, and admin task that are on my to-do list
- Block 3: 11:30 a.m.–12:45 p.m. – lunch with a potential client
- Block 4: 1–2 p.m. – coaching call
- Block 5: 2:15–3:45 p.m. – shoot a leadership video
- Block 6: 4–5 p.m. – emails, administrative tasks for project
- Block 7: 5–6:15 p.m.– go to the gym
- Block 8: 6:15 p.m. onwards – family time

You will have between twenty to thirty blocks of time to accomplish your work in a five-day 9–5 work week. When you look at your week from this point of view, you are less likely to overestimate what you will be able to achieve in a week. By blocking my week, I'm able to maintain my focus on one project (or type of project) at a time before moving on to the next.

If you don't control your schedule, it will control you. Give it a try this week. First, create a list of things you would like to accomplish this week. Next, put an estimate of how much time you think it will take to complete that task. Here is an example:

- Plan team devotional – 1 hour
- Plan fall ministry schedule – 2 hours
- Email Jim G – 5 minutes
- Write a thank-you note to Alice B – 5 minutes

- Staff meeting – 75 minutes
- Listen to Tony Morgan podcast – 45 minutes
- Lead worship rehearsal – 90 minutes

Batch items into similar categories. Many of the smaller items on your list can be batched together. Here are a few of mine: Administration (Emails, Filing, etc.), Meetings, Creating, Coaching, Planning, Personal Growth, Family, Exercise. I have these color-coded in my Google Calendar, so I can get a visual image of my week in one glance. Insert blocks on your calendar, and insert the specifics of what you will accomplish during that time. Now you have a built-in method for seeing how you are investing your time.

Tip #6: Build a Defense System Against Distractions

Distractions are deceptive. You start your day knowing the most important things you need to achieve. But as you launch into your top priority, you get a text from a co-worker asking if you can talk for five minutes.

The battle begins.

You reason, *This will only take a few minutes. They are depending on me to respond quickly. I know I need to talk to them today, so I might as well get it out of the way now.* So you drop everything and respond. Before long, your whole day is spent reacting to those around you.

Your ability to defend your priorities against distractions determines the level of your productivity on any given day. And it seems most people's defense systems are weak.

When I lose the battle with distractions, one of these three factors is usually at the root:

i. **Immediate gratification**—Responding gives me more satisfaction than the current priority task I am working on.

ii. **People Pleasing**—I respond so the individual will like me or not be upset with me.

iii. **The easier option**—Responding to the distraction is less effort than the priority task I am working on.

Distraction is the opposite of traction. Traction is what you need to make significant progress toward your goals and mission. If distractions consistently win the small battles, you will lose the ultimate war—accomplishing your priority goals.

So you need a Distraction Defense System (DDS). A good DDS has three elements:

- **Treat a priority like a priority**

There are plenty of days I write down my top three priorities but fail to accomplish them. It's not what I say that determines my priorities; it's what I act on.

Imagine you were with the president. During that meeting, you get that same text from a co-worker asking if you could talk for five minutes. You wouldn't dream of responding until later. Meeting with the president is the most important thing you could be doing at that moment.

The same applies to your priorities for the day. If you block out an hour for exercise and someone asks you to meet during that hour, you will say "no" if it is indeed a priority.

- **Know your enemy**

I have come to look at distractions as my enemy. They try to steal that which is most important to me. What distracts me may not be a distraction for you. You have to know your own vulnerabilities. The most common distractions include texts, phone calls, social media, surfing the internet, email, co-worker dropping by, working in a noisy environment.

It's funny when I look objectively at this list of enemies. None of them are more important than my priorities for today, which include

- o writing a chapter for my new book
- o shooting a training video
- o going to the gym
- o contacting a couple of clients
- o playing with my grandkids.

What you do with a distraction actually says a great deal about how important your priorities really are.

■ **Grow your ability to focus**

Many people say, "I just can't focus." The truth is, we all can. But you have to learn how. Focus is a skill that can be developed. In fact, it is a crucial skill if you want to maximize the time God gives you on this earth.

I define focus as *Knowing what is essential at the moment and bringing full attention to move it forward.*[5]

Let's take a quick yes/no test.

- o Do I know my top three priorities for today?
- o Did I win the battle against distractions yesterday?
- o Did I make significant progress toward my big goals/ objectives/projects?

How did you do? These questions should be used to help you determine your focus and keep it there.

What are the biggest distractions you typically face? Make a list of your top three.

What can you do to defend yourself against those?

Tip #7: Evaluate and Recalibrate

Do you ever find yourself frustrated, wishing you could get more accomplished? You work long hours but go home with a task list that seems longer than it did when you went in that morning. So you lock up the office and tell yourself you will put in a few extra hours tomorrow to catch up.

But working longer hours isn't the solution.

How do I get more done? is a question most of us ask ourselves consistently. But there is a more important question: *Why do I not get more done?*

Before you look for a solution for how to do more, it would be wise to understand why the problem exists in the first place.

Jesus said, "My yoke is easy and my burden is light" (Matthew 11:30). A yoke is a wooden frame created to fit over the shoulders of two oxen harnessed in such a way that they can pull a plow together. The picture Jesus is giving is one of a young ox yoked to a plow alongside a mature ox. The stronger ox bears the weight, while the young ox stays in step to accomplish the work alongside the mature one. Two things happen for the young ox: i. He learns how to plow; and ii. He isn't overburdened by the weight.

That doesn't mean life and work will always be easy, but it does mean that when we stay in tandem with Jesus, the stress of work and ministry should not wear us down.

Here are a few startling statistics about those who are in full time ministry:

1,500 clergy leaving pastoral ministry each month. – The Barna Research Group

90% of clergy in all denominations will not stay in ministry long enough to reach the age of retirement. – U.S. Bureau of Labor and Statistics

50% of pastors indicated that they would leave the ministry if they had another way of making a living. – Hartford Institute for Religious Research[6]

Why is this the case?

Perhaps we've taken off the yoke and are going a direction Jesus isn't asking us to go. We might be doing some or all of the following:

- I am allowing other people to set the agenda for my day.
- I am allowing unnecessary distractions.
- I am not planning my day and missing the important things God is calling me to do.
- I am trying to please people.
- I have not learned to say "no."
- I am failing to trust team members around me with tasks or projects.
- I am trying to prove myself to someone.

If my workload is overwhelming me, then I have to ask these questions. It happens to me regularly, so here are some questions to help me re-yoke and get back in step with Jesus.

- Am I allowing things into my schedule that God has not asked me to do?
- Am I operating primarily from God's plan for me or from other's agenda for me?
- Do I begin each day by identifying the three WINs of the day?

Conclusion

Ministry can be demanding. And if you drift from your mission, you may well find yourself drifting from your original passion for Christ as well. There are seasons in ministry that are exceptionally busy, but they should be the exception, not the rule. So use the seven tips in this module to guard your soul and maximize your mission.

I find there are four dangers when I don't build margin into my schedule.

Danger #1: I Make Decisions I Regret

When I'm in a hurry I tend to make bad decisions. This week, I made a quick decision that I looked back on and regretted. It was a small decision that seemed inconsequential, but a bunch of bad, small decisions will eventually lead to big trouble.

Danger #2: I Miss Valuable Leadership Learnings

Solomon said in Proverbs 1:20, "Wisdom calls aloud; she raises her voice in the public square." Each day we can gain leadership wisdom. But if we haven't built margin into our schedule to think and reflect, we'll miss valuable learning opportunities.

Danger #3: I Lose My Passion

Even though I spend my days doing the very thing I love, if I don't have margin, I find myself losing my enthusiasm. For me, scheduling "Think time" is like pulling up to an emotional filling station. Stopping and reflecting on what God is doing gets me excited, encourages me, and fuels my passion. I just can't lead on an empty tank.

Danger #4: I Have Nothing to Give

If I am not growing as a leader then I will not influence the growth of the team around me. As a leader I have a responsibility to my followers to make sure I'm building margin into my schedule and growing every day.

Put It Into Practice

Choose one or more of the following to complete prior to meeting with your trainer.

1. Research how to write a life mission statement. Write a one-sentence mission statement and present it to those who know you best to get their feedback. Share what you learned with your trainer.

2. Meet with someone who leads the area of ministry you lead or aspire to lead. Ask them the following questions, and discuss what you learned afterward with your trainer.
   a. How do you prepare for your week?
   b. What is the biggest time management challenge in your area of ministry?
   c. What things are most important to delegate to others in this area of ministry?
   d. How do you deal with people in your ministry who habitually waste your time?
   e. What advice do you have for me about managing my time?

3. Practice time blocking by blocking out your 9–5 for the upcoming week. Put meetings, tasks, and projects in sixty- to ninety-minute blocks on your calendar. Review this with your trainer at the beginning of the week. Then evaluate it with your trainer at the end of the week.

4. Keep a time log of how you spend your time for a full week. Include your times of solitude and sabbath so you can evaluate not just how you are spending your work time, but how well you are practicing silence and solitude. Journal what you learned from the experience.

5. Practice identifying your three WINs for each day. Do this for a full week, and discuss with your trainer what you learned from this experience.

Reflect on Your Learning

Where did you grow the most in this competency?

What next step do you need to take to continue to grow in this competency?

Meet With Your Trainer

Consistent practice can be a great beginning to sharpening a skill, but developing a skill also requires processing what you learned with others. Meet with your trainer and discuss what you learned from this module.

Dig Deeper

If you are participating in an internship or want to continue to grow in the competency of time management, go to www.maclakeonline. com/internshiptools to download the companion guide to this book.

---

[1]   Stephen R. Covey, A. Roger Merrill, Rebecca R. Merrill, *First Things First* (New York: Free Press, 1994), 94.

[2]   See Ward Cushman, "There's A Place For Solitude In All Our Lives," *To Every Nation*, https://toeverynation.com/6-times-when-jesus-chose-solitude-over-people/.

[3]   Marcus Buckingham, *Go Put Your Strengths to Work: 6 Powerful Steps to Achieve Outstanding Performance* (New York: Free Press, 2007), 165–211.

[4]   Peter Drucker, *The Effective Executive: The Definitive Guide to Getting the Right Things Done* (New York: Harper Collins, 1967), 35–37.

[5]   If you want to grow in your ability to focus, here are two book recommendations: Cal Newport, *Deep Work: Rules for Focused Success in a Distracted World* (New York: Grand Central Publishing, 2016); Gary Keller with Jay Papasan, *The One Thing: The Surprisingly Simple Truth About Extraordinary Results* (Portland, OR: Bard Press, 2013).

[6]   See Julie Maxwell, "Why Pastors Leave the Ministry by Fuller Institute, George Barna and Pastoral Care Inc.," *Shepherds Watchmen*, August 11, 2019, https://shepherdswatchmen.com/browse-all-posts/why-pastors-leave-the-ministry/.

3

Decision Making

The decisions you make as a ministry leader will make or break your credibility with your team. As long as you are making good decisions, your choices go largely unnoticed. But the moment you make an unwise decision, or what others deem to be a wrong decision, it raises concerns. And often these concerns are well founded.

I once had a young student director on my staff who made a naïve, bad decision. Within thirty minutes my phone was ringing off the hook with calls from upset parents. The next evening, we gathered all the offended parties and worked to bring understanding and unity. Although we were able to bring resolution to the situation, it didn't go without cost. It took a long time before parents would fully trust this staff member again.

Making decisions can feel risky. When I find myself struggling to decide, often it's not because I don't know what to do. It's because I'm fearful of how a particular person or group will respond. For example, you know you need to cut the budget by 20 percent, but your team will not be happy about it. Or you know the right thing is to ask a long-standing volunteer to step away from your ministry area, but you suspect they're not going to go quietly. And in recent years, decision making has only become more complicated in the face of a global pandemic and political unrest.

Anticipating the responses of others can create an added pressure in the decision-making process, especially when dealing with two well-meaning, mature people who hold polar opposite opinions on what they think should or should not happen. This sense of anticipation can lead to emotional turmoil and delay an inevitable outcome. Making the right decision too late is just as bad as making a wrong decision.

The wrong decision or the delay of a proper decision can lead to

- Damaged trust
- Hurt feelings
- Loss of time or money
- Team members feeling dishonored

The list could continue.

When David wrote Psalm 86, we don't know what he was experiencing, other than that his enemies were attacking him. But in this psalm, he pens a song affirming his dependence on God. In verse 11, he writes, "Teach me your way, LORD, that I may rely on your faithfulness; give me an undivided heart."

David asks that God teach him his way. The Hebrew word for "teach" was frequently used for "pouring water" or "pouring rain." David is asking God to pour out his wisdom and instruction on him, so he can better rely on God's faithfulness. In doing so, David knows this wisdom will keep him from having an undivided heart and help him make wise decisions as Israel's leader.

In his book *Ask It*, Andy Stanley focuses on one question that will help you make better decisions: *In light of my current circumstances, what is the wise thing to do?*[1]

As you go through this session, think of several decisions you need to make. I will be giving you six questions to consider, which will help you to make wise decisions. As you encounter each question, think about your decisions through that particular lens. Go ahead and write two of these big decisions in the blank here. This will give you something to look back on as we move through the content.

In this module, we will focus on deepening your discernment and developing your competency of making decisions.

First, let's work to define our terms:

Character: *Discernment*

Leaders recognize and respond to the presence and activity of God.

Competency: *Making Decisions*

Weigh a variety of options to make a prayerful, wise choice that reflects God's desired outcome.

Objectives

1. Practice sharpening your discernment.
2. Process a decision you are struggling with through the grid of four reasons people get stuck in decision making.
3. Make a list of your life values and use them to make a personal decision.
4. Give a decision away by empowering an individual or a team to make that decision.
5. Gain decision-making wisdom by learning from an older, wiser leader.

Deepen Your Character: *Discernment*

Something felt "off." I couldn't quite put my finger on it. After the worship service, a man who was new to our church approached and asked if he could meet with me about some concerns over our ministry. The disturbing feeling in my soul wouldn't leave, so I asked another staff member to sit in with me as a witness.

That afternoon, the man walked into my office and told my friend and me to turn off our phones and give him our full attention. He opened an envelope and said God had spoken to him regarding our church. He requested that we sit, listen, and not talk until he finished. From there, he proceeded to read a six-page letter, in which "God" gave a scathing criticism of every aspect of our ministry.

When he finished, the other staff member and I sat a little dumbfounded by his accusations and characterization of our ministry. If we took this letter at face value, it was a clear sign that God was not happy with anything we had been doing.

However, rather than be discouraged, we both felt a sense of God's presence that guided a gentle response. We thanked the man for his willingness to confront us even though we disagreed with his assessment. We told him we wanted to be open to any truth in his criticism, that we would pray, and if God revealed any necessary changes, we would act on those. But then I said, "Sir, you are new to our church, having only attended twice. While I want to be a leader who is always open to feedback, I would advise you to take the time to get to know people before confronting them. You don't know anything about me, my life, history, or motives. Yet, you took it upon yourself to levy severe accusations against me. Because you confronted me without showing any interest in knowing me, it isn't easy to respect your opinions."

In our flesh, we wanted to dismiss this man, or to be defensive or argumentative. We wanted to lash back and be vengefully critical of his approach. But the Holy Spirit somehow grabbed our hearts and helped us see that this man was wounded and dangerous, and dismissing him or arguing with him would not serve any purpose. Responding in a gentle but firm manner seemed to disarm the man. He walked out, and we never heard from him again.

When leading a ministry, you will face criticism, challenges, and spiritual warfare that can dishearten and distract you from your mission. But allowing God to shape a spirit of discernment in your character can help guard against spiritual missteps.

Ruth Haley Barton defines discernment as "the capacity to recognize and respond to the presence and activity of God—both in the ordinary moments and in the larger decisions of life."[2] This skill does not come naturally for anyone. Because of our sinful nature, our default impulses are to look out for, defend, or protect ourselves. But discernment leads us to be guided by the presence and power of God in a moment.

Scripture

As you read the following Scripture, meditate on what the author wishes to communicate, and answer the questions below. Allow the Holy Spirit to speak to you and challenge you as a leader so that you can grow in discernment in your everyday life.

Romans 12:2

Do not conform any longer to the pattern of this world, but be transformed by the renewing of your mind. Then you will be able to test and approve what God's will is—his good, pleasing and perfect will.

What "patterns of this world" do leaders tend to conform to the most?

Which one is the biggest challenge for you?

How would you describe the process of being transformed?

In what area of your life or leadership do you need God to give you greater discernment right now? In what ways can you "test and approve" his will?

Now that we have examined the character trait of discernment, we can begin to work through the core competency for this module: *Making Decisions—weigh a variety of options to make a prayerful, wise choice that reflects God's desired outcome.* As you read what follows, note how discernment can undergird a leader's competency of making decisions.

Develop Your Competency: *Making Decisions*
Preassessment

Before proceeding, complete the assessment below. In the final module of this training guide, you will retake it as a postassessment to measure your transformation and growth in this competency.

The following proficiencies demonstrate mastery of this module's competency. For each of them, give yourself a grade of A, B, C, D, or E to reflect your actual level of competency today. Giving yourself an A+ indicates you are a model for others to follow. An E indicates no mastery.

Proficiency	Preassessment
I ground all my decisions in prayer and God's Word.	
I give appropriate consideration to others' advice and wisdom in decision making.	
I seek out as much information as possible and make decisions in light of the appropriate information.	
I understand how the past, present, and future can influence decisions.	
I display courage to make wise decisions even when it may not be the popular thing to do.	

Reflection Questions

What's the most difficult decision you've had to make as a leader?

What did you do well in the way you processed and made that decision?

What would you do differently?

In which of the proficiencies above do you need to grow the most?

The Dangerous Maybe

Have you ever been leading a meeting and found yourself commenting on an idea or suggestion saying, "Yeah, maybe we should do that," but then move past it without any action steps? "Maybe" is a dangerous word in the vocabulary of a leader. It implies uncertainty, lack of direction, unclear priorities, and indecision.

First, it *damages the execution process*. When the leader says "maybe," everyone has to wait until the final decision is made before they can take action. If the decision is critical to the organizational goals or project, then it creates delays and frustration for team members.

"Maybe" also *damages team alignment*. When the leader says "maybe," some people in the room hear "yes," while others hear "no." Team members then move into action based on their assumptions rather than in alignment with their mission and each other. When you have people going in different directions, it always creates chaos and conflict.

Next, it ***damages individuals' confidence***. When people share ideas or suggestions publicly, they're making themselves vulnerable. So if the leader says "maybe" to their idea, without adequate explanation, it can be perceived that the idea was rejected and their input isn't desired. If the individual feels devalued by the leader's "maybe," they may choose not to offer input in the future.

Finally, "maybe" ***damages leadership credibility***. Some leaders have "maybe" as a default setting, enabling them to procrastinate and avoid uncomfortable ideas and input. Followers will eventually recognize this delay pattern, and the leader will lose the respect of his or her team. The leader will be perceived as one who is unable to get things done.

One of the hardest parts of leading a ministry is making difficult decisions, particularly the kinds of decisions that shape your entire ministry area. I've heard it said that 95 percent of the decisions made by senior leaders could really be made by a sixth grader, but it's the final 5 percent that are the tough decisions. Regardless of what level of leadership you're at, there are times when you will face tough decisions. And it's when we face those tougher decisions that we can often get stuck.

What do you do when you face a great opportunity, but it comes with great risk? What do you do when a key leader has become toxic and is subtly damaging the organizational culture? What do you do when finances take a downturn and you have to reduce staff? Those are the kinds of decisions that can paralyze leaders.

Making bold decisions will require the type of courage that Moses called Joshua to embody as he led the people into the Promised Land (Joshua 1). This is not natural courage. It's given by God, and it's necessary for the task. God knew what would be required for Joshua to lead the people. In the same way, God knows the tough decisions that you and I will face on our leadership journey, and he's willing to supply the courage we need.

Here's the thing I know: when the organization is stuck and a decision needs to be made, people are watching to see what you will do. Everybody knows you're stuck; everybody knows momentum has gone backwards. So you know you have to deal with it. But sometimes making the hard decision to get the ministry unstuck feels impossible. If you don't make the decision, it just keeps lingering. If you don't make the decision, in essence you *are* making a decision. And not making a decision can often be the most dangerous decision we can make.

So let me give you six important questions to ask as you learn how to make wise decisions.

Question #1: What Am I Hearing God Say?

One of the challenges of making tough decisions is looking in the wrong direction for the wrong reason. You can look back at the past out of fear. You can look to others to try to please them. You can look to your own strength to try to figure out a plan of action.

Sadly, Christians far too often look everywhere but to God to determine what decision they need to make. Sometimes our familiarity with God can mean we fail to really listen to what he is trying to say to us. As we get older and more experienced, it becomes increasingly tempting to rely on our own intellect. Obviously, God grows our intellect and wisdom, and they are useful tools. However, God wants us to remain in constant dependence on his wisdom and his way.

If you take a quick look at Acts 15 and 16, you will see the Holy Spirit providing direction for leaders in two very different ways. First, in Acts 15 the apostles were debating the necessity of circumcision for salvation. Apparently there were those who were teaching that although faith in Jesus was the basis of salvation, circumcision was still necessary. Here the apostles gathered to investigate the matter together, and after a time of discussion and seeking God's purpose from the Scriptures, Luke records their conclusion with these words: "It seemed good to the Holy Spirit and to us" (Acts 15:28). There was no supernatural display of the Spirit's direction, but it was clear to the apostles that the Holy Spirit was directing them through their study of the Scriptures and in discussion with one another.

In chapter 16, however, Paul was on his second missionary journey. There's no doubt he mapped out his journey. But midway through the trip, the Holy Spirit diverts his plans and sends him to Macedonia instead. There was an obvious interruption of the Holy Spirit that made Paul's decision clear (Acts 16:6–10). Here, the activity of the Spirit isn't through conversation or time in the Word but is a more direct leading. Luke says, "the Spirit of Jesus would not allow them to" (v. 7). We're not told exactly how the Spirit prohibited this, but it was a clear, spiritual direction that Paul and his companions received.

As a ministry leader, you must remain dependent on the Holy Spirit as you lead. There will be times you will feel the pressure to decide, yet something is unsettled in your spirit. In that case, commit more time to prayer, godly counsel, and seeking God's will through his Word. Other times we can trust that the Spirit of God will impress upon our minds the direction we need to take. Although you may not feel 100 percent certain of the decision, you can have peace about it if you've sought the Lord and genuinely desire to follow his prompting.

Question #2: Why Am I Struggling With This Decision?

Let me give you four reasons we get stuck in decision making, which will then help us learn how to move forward and make wise decisions.

- **Confusion:** *I have too many options*

There are so many pathways you could take, and you're looking at four, five, six options. The more options you have, the more details you have to sort in your mind, the more potential outcomes emerge, and you quickly find that you just get stuck.

- **Lack of courage:** *I am afraid to make the decision*

You know that if you make the right decision a key person is going to get upset; or the decision to seize an opportunity comes with risk, and you don't have the courage to make the decision, so you just keep putting it off. It's important to be honest here—sometimes we blame shift our indecision rather than face up to our own fear.

- **Desiring unanimous consensus:** *I want everyone to agree*

In my first year of full-time ministry, an influential leader in the church approached me on a Sunday morning. It was obvious he was not happy. He began to explain how he disagreed with a decision I made regarding something we did in the worship service. I patiently listened and then told him I was sorry he did not appreciate that element of the service. Then I said, "You know, it is impossible to please everyone in such a diverse congregation." I will never forget his response: "Your job is to figure out how to please every member of this church."

Wow! Talk about setting someone up for failure. As leaders, we need to be open to input, but then we must make a choice. And often there will be a number of people who will disagree with your decision. If you are striving for 100 percent consensus, you may be waiting a long time to make decisions.

- **Uncomfortable with change:** *I feel anxious about change*

The person most comfortable with change is typically the leader. In many cases, ministry leaders get to pray, process, and plan change earlier than anyone else on the team. But sometimes we are forced to change even though we may be uncomfortable with it. A directive from a senior leader, a culture shift, or an unforeseen circumstance may cause a necessary change in your ministry.

When the global pandemic hit in 2020, every ministry area had to change the way they operated. During that time, as I coached pastors and staff all across the US, I noticed how uncomfortable many of them were with how they were forced to adapt. Some navigated this time like a champ. But others complained, resisted, and dreaded the changes. As a result, the teams under their leadership struggled with the changes as well.

Which of the reasons above do you typically struggle with the most?

How has that hurt your leadership in the past?

Question #3: What Do I Need to Help Me Move Forward to Make a Decision?

Now, let's go back and look again at the reasons we are stuck. Let me give you some tips on each of these to discern exactly what it is that you need to move forward.

- **If you're stuck because of *confusion***

In this case you're probably stuck because you have multiple solutions to choose from. To get unstuck, you need to find some time to get away and have space by yourself, or with your key team members, to process and think.

Take a giant Post-it or a legal pad and make a list of all your options. On a separate Post-it or legal pad page, write out the core values of your church. This is crucial because as you process the decision, you want to make sure it is based on your core values or what I call "core behaviors." Write out the pros and cons under each option. Look at each option and based on your core values and the pros and cons, pray about what God is leading you to do and make a decision to do it.

The great baseball coach, Yogi Berra, famously suggested, "When you come to a fork in the road, take it." Here are some questions that might provide help as you work toward greater clarity.

- **Do I need more clarity on our vision?** The direction of where you are headed in the future can have a significant impact on your decisions. Sometimes we lose sight of the vision and make decisions that do not align well with where we are headed.

- **Do I need more clarity on the options?** Sometimes a lack of facts makes decision making fuzzy. So simply ask, "What further information do we need that will bring greater clarity to our situation?"

■ **If you're stuck because of a *lack of courage***

We're afraid that people are going to get upset, or a key person is going to quit if we make the tough call. So the most important thing you can do is talk to your key influencers first and get their perspective, their buy-in, and make sure they're supportive.

One of the worst mistakes I made in my first two years of church planting was making tough decisions without the wise counsel and support of my elders. They finally came to me and said, "We have agreed with your decisions but not everyone does, and we can't protect you and support you if you don't include us." That was a wake-up call for me.

If you have the buy-in from your key leaders, it's not such a big deal if one person is upset. But it is a really big deal if your key leaders don't know, or don't support, the decisions you've made. You must have the courage to make the decision. But if you're going into a fight, I've always found it helpful to do it with a few friends.

■ **If you're stuck because you're *desiring unanimous consensus***

Here we're afraid to make a decision because we think everybody has to agree. If you're constantly leading by consensus it is going to cause more division than unity. Here's why: People are different; they have different perspectives, different opinions, and different preferences. If you have a tough decision to make it's great to get input from others. But ultimately you make the decision based on the mission, vision, values, and senior leadership structure of the organization, not the overarching opinion of people.

If you always try to lead by consensus, you will be switching directions all the time. So ask for input, but don't focus on consensus.

Remember:

- o It's more important the decision is made based on the values of the organization than the vote of the people.
- o It's more important the decision is made based on the priorities of the organization than the preferences of the people.
- o It's more important that decisions are made in view of the mission of the organization than going with the mood of the majority.

Don't wait to gain consensus. Pray, get the best wisdom, and make the tough call.

- ■ **If you're stuck because you're *uncomfortable with change***

If you don't get comfortable with change, you better get comfortable with not being relevant, because if you're not changing, you're not going to remain relevant. Change is inevitable for leaders. That doesn't mean you have to like change, but it does mean you have to learn to lead through change.

So what do you do? Our team always says, "We don't make changes; we make upgrades." That shift of language really does help. If you're uncomfortable with big changes, then what are some small upgrades you can make? Keep stretching yourself, and you will gradually become more comfortable and see the value of making changes.

There will be times as a team or as an organization when you get stuck or you get knocked backwards. But it's in those times you have to clear your head and be decisive, so you don't lose the confidence of your team. When facing a tough situation or a big decision, I've learned over the years to ask myself, "What would a leader I admire do in this circumstance?" Ask yourself that question. Answer it, and then go do that.

Go back to the two big decisions you wrote down at the beginning of the module. Write them down again below.

What are you not acting on that you need to act on?

What's holding you back?

What do you need to do this week in order to move that decision forward?

Question #4: What Decision Best Fits Our Values?

Filter your decisions through values. For example, when you are considering how to spend your budget, you should do this through the lens of your values.

This point was once driven home to me when I took a young church planter I was mentoring with me to a conference where I was speaking. While there, this planter got a call that someone had given seventy thousand dollars to the church. He was obviously elated. I knew we'd spend the entire ride back to the airport—some two hours—talking about how he was going to use that money.

When we got in the car, I brought it up. "How are you going to spend the money?" I asked. His reply was predictable. He was a planter without a building, so he said he'd probably put most of it in savings so that they had a solid foundation to invest in a long-term facility one day. Not a bad answer, right?

But then I started to probe a bit. I asked him to tell me his church's values, and he listed off five values. I asked him to go through each value and say how he would spend the money if he were investing directly in that value. For example, one of his values was multiplication, so I wanted to know how he would spend seventy thousand to aid multiplication. He described how he would start a church-planting residency program and build a system for reproduction in his city.

The next value he described was compassion. So I asked how he would spend the money in a way that expressed their value of compassion. The church had the beginnings of a viable ministry to the homeless in the city, and he knew that seventy thousand would make a huge difference in getting that ministry moving and seeing these men and women in need taken care of by the church.

Then we moved to the next value—life on mission. This time he talked about how they could help a couple of their members who were passionate about using business as mission to start a coffee shop to serve the city and provide a foundation for evangelism.

After going through each of the five values, he'd not once mentioned a building. You see, this planter's initial response would mean using the money for good purposes but not for purposes that were informed by his values. His decisions were shaped by what seemed pragmatically wise rather than what aligned with his values. In the same way, we all must filter our decisions through our values lest we squander the gifts that come to us in the form of time, money, or people in our ministries.

Write a list of the personal values you have for your life.

Next, process a personal decision you are wrestling with, using your values.

How did filtering the decision through your values help bring clarity to the decision?

Question #5: Am I Really the One Who Should Be Making This Decision?

A common mistake among young leaders is to think their job is to make all the decisions. That's what leaders do, right? Wrong. Leaders don't make all the decisions.

After working for the North American Mission Board one year, I pulled my team of seven together to make an announcement. "You all have been with me for a full year now. So moving forward, you will be making more decisions, and I will be making less." I explained that each of them knew me and my values well enough that they no longer needed me to make as many decisions.

You may not be in a place to do this yet, but the point holds. If you can allow others to make the decision—based either on their role or on their gifts—then you can be freed up to make the decisions you are uniquely gifted and responsible to make. Sometimes the difficulty we face in making hard decisions is based on the fact that we don't have the knowledge required to make a good decision in that area. Or it might be that someone else on our team can, and should, wrestle with the nuances of a choice and face the consequences and challenges that might come from this decision. Not only will this free you up as a leader, but it will also empower others to take responsibility for the ministry department.

To do this well, you will need to help other people make good decisions. You can do this in two primary ways. First, you can model good decision making. That way, they pick up the patterns of the choices you make and can replicate them over time. Second, you can ask them questions as they see you making decisions. These questions could be:

- What would you have done in that situation?
- Who have you seen handle a similar situation, and how did they do it?
- What did we do that worked well, and what could have been better?

These types of questions are meant to teach people how to think wisely, and when they learn how to think wisely, they learn how to make better decisions without you. That is the ultimate outcome of leadership development. You know you've done your job when the people you lead no longer need you.

Unfortunately, many leaders have the mindset that it's their job to make all the decisions for their area of responsibility. But making too many decisions can actually damage your credibility. A leader who monopolizes the decision making for his or her team can appear controlling, paranoid, fearful, or arrogant. As a leader, your job is not to make all the decisions; it's to make the hard ones. So what do you do with all those smaller and easier decisions? Give them away!

Empowering your team to make decisions is one of the most effective ways of developing their leadership skills.

So, what is your role once you give decisions away?

- Praise them for making a wise or timely decision.
- Coach them after they make a wrong decision.
- Back them up on their decisions.
- Give them more significant levels of decision-making responsibility.
- Teach them to give away decisions.

What decisions do you need to stop making? Who will you give the decision-making responsibility to?

Question #6: What Do I (We) Need to Do to See With Fresh Perspective?

Sometimes we find ourselves in a rut: doing the same things, in the same place with the same people. This routine can limit us from seeing things from a different perspective. So, when you're struggling to make a decision and need a fresh perspective, ask yourself, *What do I (we) need to do to gain a fresh perspective?*

I once heard a story about the executives at Intel.[3] This was back in the 80s; things were going badly, and they were stuck. Andy Grove and Gordon Moore, some of the top executives, got together and discussed what they needed to do. They finally decided they needed a change in mentality, so some of the top executives got together to come up with an action plan. At one point in the meeting, Grove turned to Moore and said, "If we got kicked out and the board brought in a new CEO, what do you think he would do?" Moore's answer to this question led the pair to decide that they should "walk out the door, come back in and do it ourselves." This change in perspective gave them the mentality they needed, and they figured out what to do, and they did it. Their decisions resulted in a decade of 30 percent annual growth for the organization.

Conclusion

I've never seen a more challenging time to lead than this current season. The shifts we are experiencing in our culture mean that leaders' skills and wisdom are being challenged.

I've always said leadership is easy 90 percent of the time; it's the other 10 percent that makes you want to give up.

There will always be times leadership is difficult and requires making tough calls. That's why leaders get paid the BIG bucks! (Okay, maybe not that BIG, but you know what I mean). We have to recognize that handling challenging situations, difficult decisions, or problematic people can make or break your leadership credibility.

Put It Into Practice

Choose one or more of the following to complete prior to meeting with your trainer.

1. Think about the toughest decision facing you right now, and spend time praying for wisdom and discernment before making the decision. Seek out specific Scriptures that might relate to that decision. Write a list of options, considering the potential benefits and consequences of each option. Ask the Lord, "What is the wise thing to do?" Then commit to doing it.

2. Create a step-by-step decision-making process you can use in the future to help you make informed, well-thought-out decisions.

3. Interview a church staff member about his or her decision-making process. What did you learn? What action steps are you going to incorporate into your own life? Meet with your trainer and share what you learned.

4. Seek advice from two or three people regarding a decision you're facing. What did you learn? How well did you listen? Was the advice helpful?

5. Delegate a decision to someone on your team. Tell them why you chose them and give them the authority and support they need to make the decision. Debrief this with your trainer, and discuss what you learned by delegating a decision.

Reflect on Your Learning

In what aspect of this competency did you grow the most?

What next step do you need to take to continue to grow in this competency?

Meet With Your Trainer

Consistent practice can be a great beginning to sharpening a skill, but developing a skill also requires processing what you learned with others. Meet with your trainer and discuss what you learned from this module.

Dig Deeper

If you are participating in an internship or want to continue to grow in the competency of making decisions, go to www.maclakeonline. com/internshiptools to download the companion guide to this book.

---

[1] Andy Stanley, *Ask It: The Question That Will Revolutionize how you Make Decisions* (Colorado Springs: Multnomah Press, 2014), 35.

[2] Ruth Haley Barton, "Discernment: The Heart of Spiritual Leadership," *Transforming Center*, https://transformingcenter.org/2012/05/discernment-the-heart-of-spiritual-leadership/.

[3] See Nagesh Belludi, "Looking at Problems from an Outsider's Perspective," *Right Attitudes*, March 28, 2017, www.rightattitudes.com/2017/03/28/outsider-perspective/.

4

Communication

It happened again. I forgot. And this time it cost an extra $200.

I signed a new client in January and needed to fly to Southern California in March. But I failed to inform my assistant until the last week of February. Had I communicated this just a couple of weeks earlier, we could have purchased the ticket for $399 rather than $599.

I forgot to make the call, send the email, reply to the text, or mail out the package. Each time it was my failure to communicate that cost us.

Every time I forget to communicate information to my team, it ends up costing something. It may be a loss of money, time, influence, respect, or trust. But there is always a cost.

I have a friend who told me his church took a group of students on a mission trip. When their plane landed, they were supposed to take a bus to their final destination. But because of poor communication, there was confusion about who was supposed to purchase the bus tickets. As a result, there were no bus tickets, and they experienced a significant delay.

We've all been there. If you've been a leader for more than two weeks, you have probably experienced the implications of a failure to communicate.

A failure to communicate, or to communicate well, will cause significant problems for a team. The Oxford Dictionary defines communication as "the imparting or exchanging of information." Zzz. Sorry, I fell asleep! If that is how you define communication, it may explain why you are not good at it.

Communication is so much more than the imparting or exchanging of information! It's also imparting who you are—your attitudes, mood, emotions, opinions, preferences, and bias. Transferring information is part of communication, but there's far more to it than just stating facts. Sometimes, it's our failure to communicate at all that hinders our leadership. Other times it's a failure to communicate the right information—we get the facts wrong and lead people astray. Still other times, we get the words right, but we do so with the wrong tone. Communication is the currency of leadership, but it's difficult to spend it well.

Paul advises us to check our spirit or our attitude in the communication process. He writes, "Let your conversation be always full of grace, seasoned with salt, so that you may know how to answer everyone" (Colossians 4:6).

In this session, you will learn fundamental principles for becoming an effective communicator. But before we jump into that, it would be wise to consider a character trait that will be of great value to you as a communicator.

First, let's work to define our terms:

Character: *Authenticity*
Leaders acknowledge they are broken and imperfect while trusting God's grace and his Spirit to conform them to the image of Christ.

Competency: *Communication*
Communicate clearly so others understand and take the appropriate action.

Objectives

1. Identify a next step to become more authentic.
2. Use the five tips to grow in your likeability.
3. Clarify what team members need to know about your personality and leadership style.
4. Practice intentional listening.
5. Assess the degree of clarity of your recent communications.

Deepen Your Character: *Authenticity*

Image management is the act of trying to be something you are not. Leaders are consistently guilty of image management, especially as they get older and their role within an organization grows. Many times, however, leaders don't have it all together, and they've not mastered the art of leading well. So they work to make other people believe something about them that's not true. People are looking for answers, advice, information, and vision. The leader knows this, so he or she feels they must strive to parade a false image.

This is especially true within ministry departments. Not only do we want to portray an image of ourselves as a competent leader, but we also know we must convey a sense of spiritual maturity and discipline that others expect from a leader in the church. We might feel frustrated, busy, maxed out, or dry, but we have to put a spin on things to make it seem like we have it all together, right? Who wants to be led by someone who seems like they don't have their act together?

On the flip side are those leaders who prize authenticity, seemingly, as a way to excuse immaturity. At times, vulnerability can be used to justify sin or unprofessionalism, especially among younger leaders.

"I wouldn't want to be a fake, so I'm just keeping it real," or so the argument goes.

God is not interested in pretense or hypocrisy. The leader who's a fraud isn't getting away with anything in the eyes of God. God sees and knows everything, and he's not interested in us using our authenticity to coddle sin either. He wants holy leaders with integrity.

So what is authenticity?

Authenticity is acknowledging you are a broken and imperfect leader while trusting God's grace and his Spirit to conform you to the image of Christ.

Authenticity means I

- try to eliminate pretense;
- acknowledge and repent of my sin;
- strive to live a holy, God-honoring life; and
- do so in full view of those that I lead.

There is something endearing and encouraging in Paul's words to Timothy when he admitted to being the worst of sinners (1 Timothy 1:15); or, when he writes to the church in Philippi, saying that he continues to strive for holiness (Philippians 3:12). Even the great Apostle Paul had not already obtained all that God had for him.

It's not like Paul was still a young leader at this point in his career. He had been trained by Rabbi Gamaliel (Acts 22:3), who was a highly respected leader in Paul's day. He had his life changed by the risen Christ in AD 36. He undertook his first missionary journey with Barnabas in AD 48, his second missionary journey in AD 51, and wrote his first five epistles from AD 52–57. It's near the end of this time that he called himself the worst of sinners, and it's even later, around

AD 62, when he writes his letter to the Philippians, saying he's still striving for more.

There's an authenticity that draws you to Paul. He even told the Philippians:

> Further, my brothers and sisters, rejoice in the Lord! It is no trouble for me to write the same things to you again, and it is a safeguard for you. Watch out for those dogs, those evildoers, those mutilators of the flesh. For it is we who are the circumcision, we who serve God by his Spirit, who boast in Christ Jesus, and who put no confidence in the flesh—though I myself have reasons for such confidence,

> Philippians 3:1–4

Leaders can easily fall into the temptation of striving to impress others or to cover up their weaknesses in order to maintain a certain image with those they lead. Rookie leaders may feel they lack credibility because of their inexperience. Older, seasoned leaders can feel insecure because of past failure or a fear of no longer being relevant. Paul built credibility by being authentic with his churches. He was both honest about his sin and passionate in his pursuit of holiness. He had nothing to hide.

Scripture

As you read the following Scripture, meditate on what the author wishes to communicate, and answer the questions below. Allow the Holy Spirit to speak to you and challenge you as a leader on how you can develop your character so that you are authentic in your everyday life.

1 Corinthians 2:1–5

And so it was with me, brothers and sisters. When I came to you, I did not come with eloquence or human wisdom as I proclaimed to you the testimony about God. For I resolved to know nothing while I was with you except Jesus Christ and him crucified. I came to you in weakness with great fear and trembling. My message and my preaching were not with wise and persuasive words, but with a demonstration of the Spirit's power, so that your faith might not rest on human wisdom, but on God's power.

Here you get a sense of the focus in Paul's leadership. Paul tells his Corinthian readers when he first came to them it was not with "eloquence or human wisdom" (verse 1). Paul didn't stroll into town trying to impress them with his knowledge or his résumé. He was intent on deflecting attention away from himself and onto Jesus Christ. He knew that Jesus, and Jesus crucified, was the only hope for the people he led.

This allowed Paul to be honest about his sin; after all, it was his sin (and ours) that necessitated Jesus' crucifixion. If Paul wanted to make much of the risen Jesus, he knew that a path to do this was to own his sin and testify to the power of God to forgive sin and overcome shame and guilt.

Additionally, Paul could trust in God's power. He intentionally downplayed his gifts so that people were not drawn to wise words, rhetorical technique, or human manipulation. He wanted people to see Jesus, so he didn't have to present a polished version of himself.

The outcome of such authenticity was people putting their faith in Jesus rather than in Paul. Isn't this what we all want—for those we lead to put their faith in Jesus rather than in us? On our best days, we know we are inadequate leaders whose role in the lives of others is limited. If you're tempted to think otherwise, just try moving to a new ministry role or location. People forget about you in short order. They might praise you today, but loyalty to leaders is often fleeting. This can either deflate us, or it can prompt us to focus on pointing people to depend on Jesus. The more people are drawn to Jesus, and the less they are drawn to us, the more we are freed to be authentic with our sin and our pursuit of Christlikeness.

What do you learn about authenticity from Paul's example?

Who is the most authentic leader you know? What would you like to emulate from their life?

In what area of your life do you find yourself most tempted to "manage your image"? How do you typically do that? What next step do you need to take to be more authentic in that aspect of your life?

Now that we have examined the character trait of authenticity, we can begin to work through the core competency for this module: *Communication—communicate clearly so others understand and take the appropriate action.* As you read what follows, note how authenticity can undergird a leader's competency of communication.

 Develop Your Competency:
Communication
Preassessment

Before proceeding, complete the assessment below. In the final module of this training guide, you will retake it as a postassessment to measure your transformation and growth in this competency.

The following proficiencies demonstrate mastery of this module's competency. For each of them, give yourself a grade of A, B, C, D, or E to reflect your actual level of competency today. Giving yourself an

A+ indicates you are a model for others to follow. An E indicates no mastery.

Proficiency	Preassessment
I consistently display a positive attitude when communicating.	
I ask questions and listen in order to ensure communication has been clear.	
I help team members understand and appreciate my personality and communication style.	
I strive to bring clarity to team members regarding the big picture, as well as details they need to be aware of to do their job.	
I demonstrate a willingness to take responsibility and apologize when appropriate.	

Reflection Questions

How do you think your family would rate your communication on a scale of 1–5, with 1 being low, 5 being exceptionally high? How about your team? Co-workers? Boss?

Where do you need to grow in your communication skills?

Principles of Effective Communication

As I was about to cross the street, I nearly stepped out in front of a bus. Seriously. I've crossed a street thousands of times in my life. But not like this. It was my first time in Scotland, and as I'm sure you know, they drive on the opposite side of the road. While I'm accustomed to looking to my left, I'm not used to looking to my right. So with a quick glance to my left, I began to take a step, just as a giant commuter bus nearly ran me over.

Communication is like crossing a busy street. You've probably been told that communication is a two-way street. I disagree. It's more like a four-way street. And you have to make sure you look in all four directions, or else you'll be hit by the bus of conflict that often comes on the backside of inadequate or unclear communication.

First, I have to look at myself to see if I am communicating all the needed information and doing so in the right spirit. Sometimes I haven't done the hard work to get the right information, or I'm intentionally withholding or slanting information to get my desired outcome.

Next, I have to look to God to ensure that what I'm communicating aligns with his will and his Word. I need to make sure that the things I'm saying are a demonstration of his truth as best I understand it and that I'm saying it in a way that models the fruits of the Spirit.

Third, I have to look in the direction of those who are listening to me communicate. I need to seek to understand them, to have a sense of what presuppositions or fears they might have that shape how they hear the message. I need to strive to communicate in such a way that the real people before me actually hear what I'm saying.

Finally, I have to look in the direction of those impacted by what I'm communicating. While the communication may not be directly with them, others may be affected. I may be communicating with one person on the team, but it can have a trickle effect on others. I need to think about the implications of my message for those who will hear it from someone else.

It's a lot to consider. But ask any leader, and they can testify to crashes caused by a failure to look in each of these directions.

The practices below are intended to help you communicate in all directions in a healthier, more effective way. When communicating to people, whether it be one-on-one, a small team, or to a large crowd, these are fundamental practices you need to keep in mind.

Practice #1: Learn to Be Likeable

Not everyone is likeable. We never think about ourselves in that category, but the truth is some leaders are difficult to like. It may be a quirk in their personality, a physical trait, or a habit. Whatever the reason, some leaders are hard to like, and this factor alone predisposes people to ignore or misunderstand the things they say.

Some may argue, "My job is not to be liked; my job is to get results." These are typically leaders who have a low retention rate of team members. It's true that leadership will often put you in positions where you are not liked or where you have to make tough decisions that harm relationships, but that doesn't mean you shouldn't care about whether or not people like you. The more they like you, as a general rule, the more apt they are to trust your leadership even when you have to make hard decisions.

A few years ago, I was studying 1 Samuel. I remember how much I liked Saul when he was first introduced in the story. He was submissive, humble, and gentle. Even after being anointed king, he went back home and farmed his land. There seemed to be no selfish ambition or unhealthy desire for power. In fact, when Samuel introduced Saul to the people, Samuel turned around and Saul was nowhere to be found! He was hiding among the luggage. If anything, Saul seemed to be avoiding a position of power.

We all know how that story turned out. Eventually Saul turned into a power hungry, insecure egomaniac who struggled to value those around him. Over time, Saul changed, and so did his leadership among the people. He went from being a likeable young man to a train wreck waiting to happen.

Now don't misunderstand me; I am not saying your motivation is to be liked. But I am saying that a key factor, or method, for effective leadership is to be likeable. There is a difference. If I am driven by a motivation to be liked, then I will make choices based on the goal of being liked. But if my method is to strive to be a likeable person, I am considering what others need in order to be receptive to my leadership.

Believe it or not, likeability is key to effective communication.[1]

Think about the type of person you enjoy being around. There are some traits that attract you to people. Being aware of these will help you behave in ways that are likeable because you know what you find likeable in others. Here are five tips to get you started on growing your likeability:

- **Have a positive attitude**

As a kid, I remember my dad telling me over and over, "Son, if you can't say something positive, it's best not to say anything at all." That is a difficult practice. It tends to be easier to be negative than positive. But a likeable person has a positive perspective on life's situations, as well as on other people.

- **Get people talking about themselves**

Have you ever gone to lunch with someone and listened to them talk about themselves for a full hour? It's not fun. You leave those lunches drained rather than energized. Work hard to avoid making conversations all about you when you are around others. Seek to end more sentences with question marks than exclamation points, especially if you are a young leader. People prefer to be asked questions than listen to bold proclamations.

- **Relate to other people's feelings or situation**

People like it when others seek to understand them. One of the best ways to do this is to acknowledge the challenges, frustrations, thoughts, questions, and common failures of those you lead, so that they are aware you actually know them and hear them. If people don't feel understood, then your message has no impact.

- **Be interested rather than interesting**

Often, we strive to get people to like us by impressing them with who we are or what we've accomplished. But the truth is, it is more effective to focus on them rather than trying to get others to focus on us. Paul teaches this concept in Philippians 2:3–4, when he writes, "Do nothing out of selfish ambition or vain conceit. Rather, in humility value others above yourselves, not looking to your own interests but each of you to the interests of the others."

- **Be enthusiastic**

Here's a great question for self-reflection: Are people drained or energized after spending time with you? If you are enthusiastic about life, then people will often be drawn to you. We all know that life can be challenging, and our ministries can seem daunting at times. But we naturally feel more confident around people who, rather than baulking at the challenge ahead, show an enthusiastic appetite to get stuck in and see things happen.

In which of the five tips above are you strongest? How do you see that strength enhancing your ability to communicate with others, particularly your team?

In which do you most need to grow? How do you see that growth area hindering your ability to communicate with others, particularly your team?

What can you do this week to grow your likeability factor?

Practice #2: Help Your Team Understand Who You Are

Some leaders attempt to maintain a "healthy" relational distance between themselves and their team. But doing so doesn't allow your team members to understand who the leader is on a personal level. This hinders communication because the words we say are always mediated through our personalities. So, people need to know something of who we are in order to make sense of the things that we say. If people do not understand who we are, then the likelihood of miscommunication is higher.

The foundation of your communication is helping your team know you. For some, this may seem like a waste of time. Why spend time letting people into your life when there is so much meaningful work to be done? The answer is simple—you'll actually get more done if people know you, trust you, and understand what you are saying.

Whenever I bring on a key volunteer or hire a new staff member, I share four things to help them get to know me.

First, *I share my mission*. My life mission statement is to encourage and equip leaders to become multipliers of multipliers. Knowing my mission helps my team understand my primary calling and motivation in life. My mission statement is a filter for everything I do. Without knowing my life mission, my team cannot see the core of who God made me to be.

Next, *I share my values*. Knowing my values helps my team understand my behaviors. I like to use the term "core behaviors" rather than values. I prefer "core behaviors" because it helps emphasize the behavioral aspect of values. Sometimes people view values as important, but they fail to make the connection between values and the daily behavior that makes those values a reality. Your values determine the way you behave and the decisions you make. When your team has insight into your values, it gives them the context to understand your choices.

Then, *I share my strengths*. This helps my team understand why I invest my time the way I do. I want to spend the majority of my time in my strengths zone. Not doing so is not good for the team or the organization. But if my team doesn't know my strengths, they may have unrealistic expectations of me or misunderstand why I prioritize certain aspects of ministry over others.

Finally, *I share my weaknesses*. Being aware of my weaknesses helps reduce my team's frustration with me. I'm an "ideas person," who loves starting new things. This means I often struggle to finish the things I start. Because my team understands that, they can encourage me, come alongside me, or challenge me when they see me struggling to cross a finish line. Also, because they know my weaknesses from the beginning of our relationship, they have more grace when I fail or fall short.

Shorten your team's learning curve in understanding who you are simply by telling them what they need to know. If you don't share your mission, values, strengths, and weaknesses up-front, they will discover them over time, but it may cost you relational equity by making them find out these things on their own.

Think back to a time you were on-boarded to a new team? What do you wish the leader had done differently that would have helped you better acclimatize?

Imagine you just recruited a new leader into your area of ministry. What are four to five things you would want them to know about you?

Practice #3: Listen More Than You Talk

Leaders like to move fast, which doesn't always lend itself to listening. A large part of leadership is understanding, discerning, reading people, assessing your culture, hearing God, and then taking action—all of which require listening. I mean, really actively listening to people. I find it interesting that in Proverbs, Solomon, who was a "get it done" leader himself, repeated the instruction, "Listen" over twenty times.

"Let the wise listen and add to their learning" (Proverbs 1:5).

"If you reject discipline, you only harm yourself; but if you listen to correction, you grow in understanding" (Proverbs 15:32 NLT).

"Those who listen to instruction will prosper; those who trust the Lord will be joyful" (Proverbs 16:20 NLT).

"Stop listening to instruction, my son, and you will stray from the words of knowledge" (Proverbs 19:27).

Solomon reminds us of the importance of such listening: "To answer before listening—that is a folly and shame" (Proverbs 18:13). Perhaps he emphasized it so much because we aren't quite as good at listening as we tend to think.

Listening is a deceptive skill. Remaining silent gives the speaker the impression we're internalizing what they say. But we all know silence doesn't always equate to listening. Being a good listener involves more than just not talking. We have to actively apply ourselves to understand the speaker and discern how we should feel, think, or act in response to what they are saying.

Sometimes we remain quiet as a courtesy, but we're not really concentrating on what's being said. Listening requires work, focus, and even discernment. Listening isn't just hearing words spoken; it's absorbing the intent of the speaker. It isn't just making eye contact; it's connecting with the soul of the one sharing. It isn't just figuring out how their words, ideas, and intentions fit into our plan, but how our resources, ideas, and gifts can fit together with theirs.

Are you listening from a "me" perspective or a "they" perspective? Here are five good reasons to listen to team members in your ministry:

- To get to know their history, story, gifts, passion, personality, or dreams

- To help them process a struggle or a victory
- To push or drive them to more in-depth discovery or development
- To discern greater levels of how you can collaborate
- To enjoy them and for them to enjoy you

If you're not genuinely listening, you're missing opportunities to improve, grow, gain wisdom, collaborate, and make a more significant kingdom impact. And, as we've already said, by listening you are building a foundation for likeability as well.

What is the telltale sign you are a good listener? Your people feel valued, respected, esteemed, appreciated, and loved.

It's always important to remember that you are relating to people and not just communicating whatever facts you need to say. Most of us have been in the room when it was clear a leader just had a bomb they wanted to drop rather than taking the time to monitor the room, love the people, and share what needed to be said with wise, emotional intelligence.

What stood out to you the most from this segment?

What makes listening a challenge for you?

Who do you need to listen to more closely? What impact might better listening have on that relationship?

Practice #4—Strive for Clarity

I'm not one to give up very quickly, but this past Christmas, there was one task that almost drove me to the point of giving up. We bought a basketball hoop for our six-year-old grandson. My job was to read the instructions and put the hoop together. Two hours into the experience, I was convinced I was on a hidden camera TV show. The instructions made no sense. When I finally completed the job, there were several unused pieces, and the rim was facing the wrong direction.

Some leaders provide as much clarity as this set of instructions. And in doing so, they create a great deal of frustration for their team. The less clarity there is, the higher the frustration. It's true in every aspect of life. As my friend Will Mancini says, "Clarity isn't everything, but it changes everything."[2]

The problem is that clarity takes effort. Just because your message is clear to you doesn't mean it will be clear to others. And when communication is unclear it makes it difficult for others to understand or follow through. As a servant leader, your role is to help your team succeed in their position. This requires you to communicate with clarity. Here are a few questions that can help to ensure you are giving your team the clarity they need:

Vision: Have I clearly articulated the short-range, mid-range, and long-range vision of our ministry area? Many times, we share the long-range vision to someone who is a short-range thinker. That leaves the individual wondering what their role is and what next step they should take. While the vision may be clear to you, they are left with a paralyzing lack of clarity.

Role: Have I communicated what I expect of them in their role? I don't know many leaders who value job descriptions. But a simple job description can be a great tool to provide clarity for those on our team. I used to give my team a copy of their job description each December and ask them to edit it based on their current reality. Role expectations can change over a one-year timeframe, so updating them can help us keep expectations aligned.

Goals: Have we agreed upon their performance goals for the next several months? Goals are another one of those items that help us have shared expectations with those we lead. Agreeing on performance goals for a ninety-day period can bring greater clarity for those we lead.

Tasks: Have I discussed all the specifics necessary for them to complete the task successfully? We cannot lead everyone the same way. For some tasks, our team needs a high degree of direction. Telling them the specifics of *what*, *why*, and *how* is just what they need. But for other tasks, especially those in which a team member is highly competent, you can delegate the task and let people run with it. When delegating a task, it's important to identify how much direction a team member needs from you to successfully accomplish it.

Deadlines: Have we agreed upon a deadline for the project, goal, or task? There are times I have delegated a project only to approach the individual a couple of weeks later asking if it has been completed. They look at me with shock and frustration because they thought they had more time to get the work done. Each time this has happened, the team member feels as if they are failing me. But the truth is I failed them by not bringing clarity around the deadline.

Accessible: Have I made myself approachable and available? As a servant leader, my role is to help my team be successful. That means I need to be available and approachable should they need my help or further clarity. More on that in module five when we talk about coaching.

One of the most important tools as you strive for clarity is to be hyperclear on the main thing you want to communicate. When information is plentiful, it is easy for those you are leading to lose focus and get lost in extraneous information. You have to manage people's attention and keep them focused on the main thing, especially in a world of sound-bite clips and YouTube videos. Your challenge as a leader is to get people to focus on the right things at the right time. Just because you are passionate about what you have to say doesn't mean people are passionate to hear what you have to say, or that they will focus on the main thing you are trying to say. Don't assume people are listening. People have other things going through their mind that distract them. So take responsibility to get their attention.

Think about your communication with the individuals, team, or group you're working with, and consider each of the following questions:

Vision: Have I clearly articulated the short-range, mid-range, and long-range vision of our ministry area?

Role: Have I communicated what I expect of them in their role?

Goals: Have we agreed upon their performance goals for the next several months?

Tasks: Have I discussed all the specifics necessary for them to complete the task successfully?

Deadlines: Have we agreed upon a deadline for the project, goal, or task?

Accessible: Am I making myself approachable and available should they need further clarity?

What did you discover about your communication skills in this segment?

Practice #5—Be Quick to Apologize

"I'm sorry."

There's great power in those two words. They can radically change a relationship, restore trust, and heal wounds. But only if they are spoken with a spirit of authenticity.

If you want to be proficient in delivering an apology, first think about what it feels like to receive an apology. We've all seen the little kid give a half-hearted apology to his sister after he punches her in the arm. That's not what we are after as leaders. We want to be authentic in owning our mistakes and admitting when we come up short or just blow it altogether.

Not all apologies carry the same weight. Some say, "I'm sorry," only because they were caught, to get someone off their back, or because they were forced into it. These are not apologies. They are statements that acknowledge the other person's displeasure but indicate the individual in the wrong is still refusing to recognize their part in the offense.

There are two primary reasons people struggle to say, "I'm sorry."

First, some leaders work to control how others perceive them and believe that apologizing presents them as a failure. They put "a spin" on their behavior to make sure people understand they heard them, but they don't really own the failure. "Oh, I'm sorry, I was tired. That's why I did that." Making excuses is a form of image management (an attempt to control how others see you). And in doing so, we are being deceptive. Or we place blame on others by saying something like, "I'm sorry you feel that way, but…" What follows the "but" is an attempt to tell them why they should not feel the way they do. Each is an effort at image management and an outcome of our fear.

Second, some struggle to apologize because they don't like acknowledging their own brokenness. To say, "I'm sorry" is to admit my weakness, fault, or sin. For some, facing the truth about ourselves is too difficult to bear. In this case, we are not only deceiving others, but we are also deceiving ourselves.

In both cases, the underlying issue is a failure to find our identity in Christ. When we live in light of God's grace, we will have the ability to deliver an authentic apology that restores harmony and trust. We don't have to crash when we let others down because we know that Jesus knows the worst about us and has forgiven our sin and covered our shame. But when our identity is not grounded in Christ, we will face great temptation to protect our image.

An authentic apology includes several elements.

First, we have to reflect on what we did, why we did it, and what went wrong. We can't do this with a rationalizing heart that attempts to prove why we're not wrong. We have to ask the Spirit to search our hearts and show us the log in our own eye.

Next, we need to sincerely own our sins or wrongdoing, even if we think some of the critique may be unfounded.

Then, we need to be sensitive to acknowledge the emotional or tangible impact our actions had on the other individual(s). If we genuinely believe the best about others, we should be willing to love them by expressing remorse to them.

Finally, we should go to them and articulate the specific change we will strive to make. As much as possible, this should be clear and tangible so that people know we are serious about growing and changing.

Leaders are responsible for shaping the team culture. They shape the culture through how they communicate. And one of the most essential communication skills you can learn is the art of apologizing. Not only will this help you grow in your personal ability to admit sin to God, but it will also affect those on your team and may help them become better at owning mistakes when they make them as well.

Is it easy or difficult for you to give a sincere apology? If it's difficult for you, how has that affected your leadership?

Is there anyone you need to apologize to right now? What is holding you back? What next step do you need to take?

Conclusion

All of us want to get better at communication. We intuitively know that leadership requires communication, and we get frustrated, discouraged, and disappointed when we don't say the things we want or when people don't hear what we say. While you may not be a speaker, you still communicate a lot to those you lead. You lead meetings, events, and training. How you communicate matters. If you are a poor communicator, it will diminish your leadership impact. So this is an area you should strive to grow in even if you think you are doing a decent job at communicating right now. The greater your ability to communicate, the greater your ability to inspire, impact, and influence your team.

Put It Into Practice

Choose one or more of the following to complete prior to meeting with your trainer.

1. Interview someone who leads the area of ministry you currently lead or are preparing to lead. Ask them the following questions about communication:

  a. What are the common practices you use to maintain healthy communication with your team?

  b. Most of the people we work with are volunteers. What challenges do you face in keeping your team of volunteers informed?

  c. What tools, apps, resources, or rhythms do you use to help communicate well with your team?

  d. What is the biggest piece of advice you would give me about communicating with my team?

2. Observe someone who leads the same area of ministry you lead or will be leading. Ask to follow them in a situation where

they are interacting and communicating with their team. Write down what you learn from seeing them in action.

3. Delegate a project or task to a team member, and ask your trainer or someone else to observe your communication and give you feedback.

4. Invite an acquaintance, team member, or potential team member for coffee to get to know them better. Practice asking questions and being a good listener. Share what you learned from this intentional listening exercise with your trainer.

Reflect on Your Learning

Where did you grow the most in this competency?

What next step do you need to take to continue to grow in this competency?

Meet With Your Trainer

Consistent practice can be a great beginning to sharpening a skill, but developing a skill also requires processing what you learned with others. Meet with your trainer and discuss what you learned from this module.

Dig Deeper

If you are participating in an internship or want to continue to grow in the competency of communication, go to www.maclakeonline.com/internshiptools to download the companion guide to this book.

---

[1] For more on the connection between like ability and communication, see Jenny Marchal, "How To Be Likeable By Improving Your Communication Skills," *Lifehack*, www.lifehack.org/411947/how-to-be-likeable-by-improving-your-communication-skills.

[2] Will Mancini, "41 Thoughts on Living With Clarity," *Will Mancini Blog*, www.willmancini.com/blog/41-thoughts-on-living-with-clarity-1.

5

Coaching Others

"My leaders just aren't committed."

"I wish my leaders would take more initiative."

"That leader didn't follow through, again."

"For some reason, they just don't seem to understand."

In my work with churches all across North America I have heard these comments, and many like them, from staff members of all types of churches—big and small and every type of denomination. At times, all leaders are faced with leading others who struggle to get the vision or do good work. This challenge is compounded when we are leading volunteers, and we don't have the carrot of pay to reward the performance we desire. We're often left to privately lament the flaws of others and wring our hands about the things we would change if we could.

So what do the statements above have in common? Each one reflects a coaching problem within the ministry. It's easy to see the weakness in others, but it's another thing to admit that there are weaknesses in our leadership. If we don't know how to help other people get better at the work God has called them to do and we've appointed them to, then we may need to learn the skills of coaching.

Most of those on our team will know when they are missing the mark and genuinely want to grow and improve. No one likes to drop the ball regularly, so if this is the case with some of your leaders, it's likely they want to change.

And, no doubt, you'd like to see things improve as well. Most ministry leaders are stressed because there is so much to do and not enough people to carry the load. We get discouraged because those on our teams are often not following through, making mistakes, or causing issues that create more work for us. We know that if they got better at their roles, it would make life easier for us as leaders, for our churches, and for those we are called to serve.

Instead of coaching their team to help them grow in their leadership competencies, many ministry leaders shrug their shoulders and accept this reality as their lot. They are either unaware of the difference coaching can make, or they feel they are too busy to provide the coaching their team needs.

Many ministry leaders default to doing so many ministry tasks themselves rather than developing their team through coaching.

One of the things I admire about Jesus is his patience in coaching his disciples. This group of twelve young men had the privilege of watching Jesus do amazing miracles and hearing him teach outstanding lessons. Yet, as I was reading through Mark's Gospel recently, I noticed how slow they were to learn. Check this out...

In Mark 4 the disciples woke Jesus up from a nap because they were afraid a raging storm was about to bring them all to an early death. Jesus spoke the word and the storm ceased. He then looked at these young leaders and said, "Why are you so afraid? Do you still have no faith?"

Just two chapters later, the disciples watch Jesus miraculously feed five thousand people from a meager five loaves and two fish. Afterward, Jesus told them to get in the boat and go ahead of him.

Once again they find themselves in a storm. The next morning Jesus walks out to them on the water, and again calms the storm. Adding an editorial comment, Mark points out their lack of faith, saying, "and the wind died down. They were completely amazed, for they had not understood about the loaves; their hearts were hardened" (Mark 6:51–52).

Two chapters later, in Mark 8, after Jesus has just miraculously fed four thousand people, he and his disciples again get into a boat. He senses they are still lacking faith. So he asks them a series of questions. Then in verse 21, Jesus remarks, "Do you still not understand?" It seems every time they were in a boat with Jesus, he had to coach them because they lacked understanding. By this point, these men have been with Jesus for over two years, and yet they still need coaching in their faith.

Jesus shows us that coaching leaders is messy, even if it isn't always that complex. And he was obviously the Master leader himself, yet he still had to invest in the painful work of coaching those on his team who were short-sighted or weak in faith. And Jesus didn't try to coach everyone. He chose twelve men and focused his efforts on this group. Jesus spent a disproportionate amount of time with these few in order to increase his impact on the many.

The same holds true for you. As a ministry leader you cannot give everyone equal time. You will likely have team members, leaders, and coach/coordinator levels under your leadership.[1] But no matter how many leaders you choose to invest in, it's important to recognize that the work will always be messy. You'll quickly find that no matter how great the team you lead, they will still need coaching to tap into their full potential as leaders.

As you move through this module, consider your current ministry team and think about some of the areas in which they need coaching.

Ask yourself what you've done in the past to help them grow and develop. Think about what you wish you could do to help them or what you know you should be doing but often neglect. These real-life examples will help you make the most out of the character and competency we will be considering together.

As you get into this session, ask yourself the following questions:

- Do I expect people to understand after only instructing them once?
- Do I default to taking care of things myself because I can do it faster or better?
- Do I let performance suffer and complain to others about it?
- Am I overworked because I take on too much instead of delegating and developing others?

First, let's work to define our terms:

Character: *Genuine Love*
Leaders respond in a patient, caring, and honest manner to those with whom they interact.

Competency: *Coaching Others*
Guide an individual through a thought process to discover insights and action steps that lead to further development in their life and leadership.

Objectives

1. Practice expressing genuine love.
2. Use the Goal Setting template to set ninety-day goals.

3. Identify next steps to grow in the Adaptive Leadership model.

4. Assess your ability to provide spontaneous feedback to your team.

5. Choose one of the relational leadership rules and put it into practice.

Deepen Your Character:
Genuine Love

In the broader world, love and leadership are not two words that are typically connected. But leaders who love their people will develop a team of people who are loyal, give their best, and give love in return.

In ministry, it's often assumed that you love people well if you are a leader. After all, why else would you get into ministry if it weren't for a genuine love for others and a desire to pursue their greatest good?

However, many leaders unfortunately fall into one of the following two traps.

Either they fail to equate leadership with love, and use people, or even take advantage of people, to get the work of ministry done. They might build big organizations or a seemingly healthy ministry, but in their wake are many broken relationships and painful, unresolved conflicts.

Or there are those leaders in the church who signed up for ministry out of a genuine love for people, but somehow along the way they lost their focus. The goalposts moved from a genuine care for the well-being of others to something that feels sterile and institutional. Now they spend their time making things happen in a back room but see little impact in the real lives of people they know.

Scripture

Paul's definition of love in 1 Corinthians is often used in wedding ceremonies, challenging couples to love each other with a selfless love. Although this passage is frequently used in regard to marriage, we must remember Paul used it to speak of how we should love each other as believers. In fact, the entire book is written to a broken church to help them grow in love and health. The principles certainly apply to marriage, but they hardly stop there.

As you read the following Scripture, meditate on what the author wishes to communicate, and answer the questions below. Allow the Holy Spirit to speak to you and challenge you as a leader on how you can develop your character so that you are growing in genuine love in your everyday life.

1 Corinthians 13:4–8

Love is patient, love is kind. It does not envy, it does not boast, it is not proud. It does not dishonor others, it is not self-seeking, it is not easily angered, it keeps no record of wrongs. Love does not delight in evil but rejoices with the truth. It always protects, always trusts, always hopes, always perseveres. Love never fails.

We can break Paul's definition of love into four categories, with several ideas in each.

First, we see Paul's love as a demonstration of care for others—it's patient, kind, and rejoices in the truth.

Second, love is selfless—it doesn't envy or boast, and it isn't proud or self-seeking.

Third, love doesn't tear others down—it doesn't dishonor, isn't easily angered, doesn't keep a record of wrongs, or rejoice in evil.

Finally, love acts in ways that help others—it protects, trusts, hopes, and perseveres.

Each category shows us that love is fundamentally others-focused.

We can apply these same categories to our work in ministry. Often, we get so caught up in the logistics of the work, that we begin to value process over people. Process is important, but the goal of our ministry efforts is always to express and demonstrate the love of God. If we don't reflect that love, it is impossible for others to see Jesus in and through our leadership.

Which aspect of love in this passage do you most easily display?

Which is a challenge for you?

Think of a team member, family member, or co-worker you may currently be frustrated with. What can you do this week to express genuine love to this individual?

Now that we have examined the character trait of genuine love, we can begin to work through the core competency for this module: *Coaching Others—guide an individual through a thought process to discover insights and action steps that lead to further development in their life and leadership.* As you read what follows, note how genuine love can undergird a leader's competency of coaching others.

Develop Your Competency:
Coaching Others
Preassessment

Before proceeding, complete the assessment below. In the final module of this training guide, you will retake it as a postassessment to measure your transformation and growth in this competency.

The following proficiencies demonstrate mastery of this module's competency. For each of them, give yourself a grade of A, B, C, D, or E to reflect your actual level of competency today. Giving yourself an A+ indicates you are a model for others to follow. An E indicates no mastery.

Proficiency	Preassessment
I see the strengths and potential of others.	
I prefer to use thought-provoking questions over simply giving advice.	
I capitalize on team members' failures and successes in order to maximize development.	
I give challenging assignments that help individuals grow.	
I observe team members in action and provide them with honest, constructive feedback.	

Reflection Questions

Who has been the best life or leadership coach you've ever had? What made them a good coach?

If you've never had a leadership coach, what do you feel like you have missed out on?

In what three ways do you feel you need to grow in your coaching ability?

Marks of a Great Coach

As I walked through the business leadership section in Barnes & Noble, a book title caught my eye and stopped me in my tracks. The book was titled *Why Employees Don't Do What They're Supposed to Do and What to do About It* by Ferdinand Fournies.[2] I was a twenty-nine-year-old leader at the time, who only had volunteer leaders who reported to me, but the book title described the pain I was feeling. I immediately bought the book, took it home, and devoured the lessons it contained.

When I finished reading the chapters that describe sixteen reasons why people don't do what you want them to do, I made a photocopy of the table of contents. I posted it on the wall beside my desk.

For the first time, I realized that when people are not doing what they're supposed to be doing, it was often my fault, not theirs! That hurt, but it was a necessary wake-up call.

Placing blame on those we lead is like a built-in default mode for most of us. When a leader's performance is off, you can find yourself complaining, criticizing, or reprimanding without stopping to think about why their performance might be off. Fournies' book gave me a tool to help assess poor performance. This, in turn, equipped me to take the appropriate steps to help those I lead.

If you're curious about the sixteen reasons, here they are:

1. They don't know why they should do it.
2. They don't know how to do it.
3. They don't know what they are supposed to do.
4. They think your way will not work.
5. They think their way is better.
6. They think something else is more important.
7. There is no positive consequence to them for doing it.

8. They think they are doing it.

9. They are rewarded for not doing it.

10. They are punished for doing what they are supposed to do.

11. They anticipate a negative consequence for doing it.

12. There is no negative consequence to them for poor performance.

13. Obstacles beyond their control.

14. Their personal limits prevent them from performing.

15. Personal problems.

16. No one could do it.[3]

When one of your leaders is missing the mark, your new default should be to ask: *Why are they not performing well? What can I do to help them?* It is your job to help coach and correct poor performance. The easy thing is to point the finger and blame them rather than find the issue and coach them.

In this session, you will learn six marks of a great coach and see why each of these marks matters for those leading ministries in local churches.

Mark #1: Great Coaches Listen and Ask Effective Questions

My friend Dino Senesi is recognized as one of the best church-planting coaches in the country. In his training he draws a stick figure representing a church planter and asks the room, "What are the voices speaking into this church planter?" This brainstorm exercise rouses up answers such as their spouse, their pastor, their board, friends, etc. Then he asks, "What voice is missing?" People come up with a few more answers, and Dino adds them to the mix. Again, he asks, "What voice is missing?" After the group has exhausted their answers, there is still one voice missing. Dino points out that most of these voices are Telling Voices—meaning that they are the kind of voices telling the planter what he or she should do. Telling Voices give encouragement, counsel, resources, or advice. What the planter needs is an Asking Voice—one that is intent on asking good questions and drawing out of the leader the concerns, questions, ideas, and dreams that are vital for lasting health and change. Asking Voices ask questions like: *What is your number one priority right now? What is the most important next step you need to take? What options do you have right now, and which option do you think is the best? Why?* Asking Voices challenge the individual to think and discover answers on their own.

I was meeting with one of my team leaders one day when she asked how I wanted her to handle a specific situation. In my mind I quickly assessed her ability to handle the situation and recognized she didn't need me to give her the answer. So I started using my Asking Voice, asking her questions.

- What do you think your options are?
- If you were to choose one of those options, which would you choose? Why?
- What are the potential drawbacks of that option?
- How does choosing that particular option reflect the values of our organization?

So then I asked, "What are you going to do?"

She said, "What do you want me to do?"

"I'm not going to tell you," I replied. "You know me, you know our values, and I trust you to make the right decision. So, make the decision, and I will back you up no matter the outcome."

It was fun to watch her go from depending on me for an answer, to a new level of confidence in her own decision on how to handle the situation—all in fifteen minutes!

Most leaders are hardwired with a Telling Voice. Your team will benefit greatly if you increasingly use an Asking Voice. They will

- sense that you genuinely love them and care about what they have to say
- be increasingly willing to be vulnerable about their hopes and fears
- gain insight into the types of questions they should be asking of others
- be motivated to engage in the work you are asking them to do
- be loyal to you in hard times because you've cared about their well-being.

When we always lead with a Telling Voice, our team becomes dependent on us for decisions. But when we lead with an Asking Voice, it equips them to make decisions.

On a scale of 1–5 (1 = low; 3 = average; 5 = a model for others to follow), how would you rank your ability to ask coaching questions?

What do you do well as a coach?

In what specific ways do you need to improve in asking coaching questions?

Mark #2: Great Coaches Agree on Performance Goals in Advance

When I was a kid, I lived across from a large, open field. It was typical for a gang of five or six of us to meet up there. Bored, with nothing to do, someone would start bragging about being the fastest among us. Then as the bravado and tension would heat up, someone would say, "Let's race!" So we would line up, and one of us would yell, "Go!" We would all take off running, but the problem was we never defined a finish line. Some would run hard for a while, but others settled into a jog or walk. Why? Because we had no idea where we were running to. It was hard to measure and hard to stay motivated when we didn't have a finish line.

Unfortunately, that's how many people are operating in their work or volunteer roles. The new year comes, and maybe the senior leader or senior pastor gives a stirring vision for the year ahead. In a sense, the gun sounds. Everyone is excited to get a fresh start. But after a short time, they get confused, tired, or discouraged because there's no sense of progress or significant contribution. So they slow to a walk or drop out of the race altogether.

I was in my mid-twenties when I first started using goals to lead my team. It didn't take long for me to get some pushback. One of the volunteer leaders on my team confronted me and explained that goal setting is a business principle and has no place in the church. Over the years, I've encountered this objection more than once.

These individuals typically point to James, which says, "Instead, you ought to say, 'If it is the Lord's will, we will live and do this or that'" (James 4:15). However, James is not talking to believers who are pursuing God's will; he is talking to those who arrogantly plan their future with selfish ambition. James is not telling us to avoid goals. He is advising us to make plans as God leads, but to hold them loosely.

Some feel goal setting is presuming we know what God wants us to do; and that if we write down goals, it keeps us from listening to the Holy Spirit. I agree; we need to remain open to where God is moving. But we also need to recognize that God involves us in the direction he is going and can communicate his direction ahead of time to us through prayer, his Word, and others' counsel.

In Luke 14:28, Jesus said, "Suppose one of you wants to build a tower. Won't you first sit down and estimate the cost to see if you have enough money to complete it?" Jesus is illustrating the importance of disciplining ourselves to think through what God is calling us to do. Anything less is unwise and irresponsible.

Goal setting is an essential element of getting results. When done correctly, goals give us motivation and a mark to run toward.

So let me get practical. Here's how I approach goal setting with my team.

Ask each of your direct reports to identify three to five priority goals they would like to accomplish in the upcoming ninety days. (By the way, I have used this with both volunteer and paid members of my team. Don't avoid goal setting for someone just because they are a volunteer.)

Many churches ask staff to set goals, but typically they are annual goals rather than quarterly. Annual goal setting has several challenges:

- Circumstances and priorities change considerably over a twelve-month period of time.
- Annual goals are rarely adjusted, adapted, or removed once they become irrelevant. As a result, you are judged at the end of the year based on goals that are no longer important.
- Many people struggle to think that far ahead, and as a result their goals are vague.

This is why I prefer quarterly goal setting. It's much easier to identify three to five priorities you'd like to accomplish over ninety days, than it is over 365 days. The shorter time frame also helps the person prioritize what is most strategic right now.

Now, I know what you're thinking. People hate setting goals. I've found the same thing. But goals challenge the team member to identify what they are trusting God to do in and through their ministry over a ninety-day period of time. When I ask team members to renew their goals for the upcoming ninety days, I like to say, "Write down three to five things you are trusting God to do in your ministry." That's a powerful question, because I don't want my team just functioning in their own strength. I want them to pray and ask, "What am I anticipating God wants to do through me?" That makes goals exciting. That makes goals relevant. It means I'm now depending on God to see these things happen. And so that's why I like statements of faith in conjunction with goals. In fact, many times I refer to goals as "statements of faith."

I prefer this language because a goal is birthed out of a conversation with God. It aligns with a passion he's put in a person's heart. As they listen to the voice of God, they're asking him what he wants to accomplish in and through them over the next three months. His answers become their goal; his answers become statements of faith … things they are trusting him to do in and through them.

Review the goals together. After a team member has submitted their three to five goals, the next step is to sit with them and review those goals. This gives you the opportunity to affirm their goals and adjust them by making them bigger or smaller. Sometimes you may need to feed back that one of their goals is not really a priority at this time, and they need to identify an alternative goal. As you review the goals, you can work together to align your expectations.

Make sure the individual doesn't confuse a goal with a task. I've seen this in teams I've led, and I've seen other leaders experience the same thing. When a team member shares their goals, it might look something like:

Goal: I'm going to recruit five new leaders.
Or something even more nebulous like:
Goal: I'm going to recruit more leaders.

Write a goal paragraph, not a goal sentence. A paragraph describes a little more what it really is they're trying to accomplish, and why they're trying to accomplish it. I try to structure these paragraphs around basic *what*, *why*, *who*, *how*, and *when* questions. So the example above would sound more like this:

Goal: I will recruit and train five new leaders to my team (*what*), in order to achieve a healthy one to five ratio, which will provide greater levels of care for my team members (*why*). I'll use the existing leaders on my team (*who*) to identify a list of twenty prospects and empower the existing leaders to have recruiting conversations (*how*), so that we can have these new leaders in place by September 6 (*when*).

This is a much more robust goal. I can see what it is they're trusting God for and why they think this goal matters.

Think about success indicators. Underneath that goal paragraph, I ask them to add success indicators. Success indicators are like milestones that show progress along the way. Ask the person to list marks that would indicate they are heading in the right direction

Success indicators for the volunteer recruitment goal might look something like this:

- Spend time praying about who to invite.
- Meet with my team to brainstorm a list of names we could potentially recruit.
- Meet with our communications team to develop a recruiting tool we can put in the hands of prospects.
- Read four articles (or videos) to develop my ability to recruit well.
- Make a list of twenty prospects.
- Enlist three of my existing leaders to help recruit the new leaders.
- Along with the three existing leaders, talk to five people each week over the next four weeks.

By using this process of goal setting, you've intentionally created a process of shared ownership. You've not just told team members what you expect of them, but you've allowed them to seek God and craft their goals based on what they feel God is saying to them. And, by presenting these goals to you as the team leader, they've invited you into the process of refining the goals, making them better, and agreeing that they are important.

When it comes to goal setting with your team members, there are three scenarios for you as a leader: First, you might look at the goals and agree with the team member on everything they've written down. Second, you might help the team member dial up or dial back the goal by telling him or her that they've either aimed too low or too high. Such a discussion helps align expectations and presses the team member to consider how they might walk out of the conversation knowing exactly what you expect. Or, third, it might be that the goal the team member has set is actually not what's important right now, and you help them reprioritize for more strategic work.

How do you feel about using performance goals in your work? Why do you feel this way?

If you had a team member question the value of setting performance goals, what would you tell them?

What is your level of experience in coaching others, based on the goals they set: No experience, little experience, or high experience?

Mark #3: Great Coaches Discuss and Agree on the Type of Input They Will Provide

Now that you've agreed on your team member's goals, it's time to agree on the type of input you will provide on each of their goals.

One of the things I learned early on in ministry is you cannot lead all people the same way. In fact, you cannot even lead an individual the same way all the time. Wise coaches adapt their approach based on the individual and the situation.

When someone on your team sets goals, there are two factors you need to consider as they work toward accomplishing them. First, how much direction you should provide. Second, the level of competency they have that will enable them to accomplish their goals.

I've put together a framework that I call the Adaptive Leadership model.

Adaptive Leadership

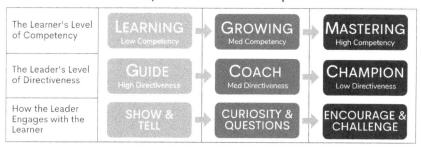

Once you agree on the goals, it's time to discuss the type of input you will provide as their supervisor. This is accomplished by discussing their level of competency with each goal and the level of direction they need you to provide. Once again, this is not something they decide by themselves; it's something you discuss and agree on.

Your team member will fall under one of three levels of competency:

The first level of competency is **Learning**. Learning means they do not have much experience or the skills necessary to fully carry out this goal.

The second level of competency is **Growing**. They may have some experience and have some of the skills but still have a gap in skills to fully accomplish that which they are trying to achieve.

The third level of competency is **Mastering**. Mastering means they have the full scope of competency needed, as well as plenty of experience that will enable them to effectively accomplish that particular goal.

Once you have agreed upon their level of competency, it then becomes clear what level of direction you need to provide.

If their competency falls into the Learning level, you need to be a **Guide**. A Guide is highly directive, telling the individual who, what, when, where, why, and how. Knowing that their competency level is low, you can give them the guidance they need to be successful.

For example, taking the goal of recruiting five new leaders mentioned above, if the individual described their competency as Learning, I would provide a high degree of direction (a Guide). In this case I might be a Guide by doing the following:

- Meet with them to help them build a list of prospects.
- Help determine who on their team would be the best recruiters.
- Invite them to follow me and watch me recruit some potential leaders.
- Send them a video on effective recruiting processes and then sit and discuss it with them.

Does this sound like micro-management? Yes, it might. And it would feel like micro-management if their competency was at the Growing or Mastering level. But it's not micro-management in this case; it's development. Because they identified themselves as Learning, they are inviting you to be highly directive.

If a team member's competency falls into the Growing level, that means you will provide **Coaching**. With Coaching, you ask questions to help them process and learn.

For example, when I meet with them one-on-one, I ask questions like:

- How is the recruiting going? What is going well? How many people have said yes? What did you do well that helped lead to that yes?
- Who has said no? Why do you think they said no? What did you learn from that experience?
- Where are you struggling? Why is that a struggle for you? What do you need to do to overcome that struggle?

I ask questions to help them reflect and learn. I try hard to not do the thinking for them but challenge them to discover for themselves. But in time, in areas where I see they are struggling, I will provide insights from my experience.

When you are providing this type of Coaching approach, your goal is to see their competency as well as their confidence grow. If I am always giving them the answers, they become dependent on me, and it ultimately cripples their confidence.

If they identify their competency as Mastering, then you need to function as a **Champion**. A Champion provides recognition and affirmation but not direction. They don't need your input because their competency is high. Of course, you can provide it if they ask for it, but only if they ask.

For example, if I were meeting with my leader whose goal is to recruit five new leaders, and they've identified their competency as Mastering, here's what I would say in those one-on-one meetings with him or her.

- Celebrate with me how the recruitment is going.
- Would you allow Jim to go with you next time you recruit a leader? I'd love for him to see you in action and learn from you.
- You're really good at recruiting others. Is there anything new you're learning about recruiting recently? I'd love to learn as you learn.

Because they identified themselves as Mastering, and I agree with that assessment, they do not need me to provide direction. Needlessly giving direction would only serve to frustrate them and make them question if I truly believe in their abilities. Sometimes I wouldn't even ask them about their goals and would instead focus on other things.

What was most helpful to you from this section?

What is your default approach: Guide, Coach, or Champion? How could learning to use the other two approaches improve your leadership?

What next step do you need to take to grow in the other two approaches of Adaptive Leadership?

Mark #4: Great Coaches Meet Regularly With Individuals for Progress Updates

No one likes to meet just for the sake of meeting, but now you've done the hard work of developing a clear plan with each of your team for ninety-day goals, your one-on-one progress update conversations get much easier.

When I meet with an individual for a progress update, there are three results I typically see. They've made **_good progress_**, they've made *little or no progress*, or they are *stuck* because they don't have everything they need.

If they've made ***good progress***, I want to ***recognize*** what they've done well and ask questions to help them learn from their progress. For example, I might ask questions like:

- Which of your strengths did you use to get this accomplished?
- Who observed you as you executed this goal? How did you leverage that for them to learn and grow in their leadership?
- What is the most important next step you need to take?

If they have made ***little or no progress,*** I want to ***redirect*** them to help them get back on track. In this case, I might ask questions like:

- What has been the biggest challenge you've faced with your goal?
- If you were to evaluate your efforts so far, what would you say you needed to do differently?
- How do you need to adjust your schedule over the next two weeks, so you can make progress on this goal?
- What is the most important next step you need to take?

If they are ***stuck*** because they don't have what they need, then I want to ***resource*** them. So I would ask questions like:

- What has prevented you from making progress with this goal?
- What do you need from me to help move this goal forward?
- Who do you know (or who can I introduce you to) who can help provide the information, wisdom, or advice you need to make progress with this goal?
- What is the most important next step you need to take?

Mark #5: Great Coaches Take Advantage of Spontaneous Development Opportunities

Is someone on your team feeling frustrated? Good!

It can be good that they are frustrated. That tells you a lot about them.

It tells you they're not content with the status quo. It tells you they're a person with a sense of drive. It tells you they're a person who sees things as they should be. They don't settle. They're not content.

As I work on my craft, my wife sometimes laughs and says, "You're never satisfied, are you?" And I'm not. Life's too short. There's too much to experience. Too much to accomplish. Of course I'm frustrated. I want more! Not more for selfish reasons. Not more for me. I want to make a better contribution. I want to make a difference for the kingdom. I want to see things move forward.

Forward progress does not happen without frustration.

In seminary, Dr. Howard Hendricks would give us challenging homework assignments that stretched our thinking as well as our abilities. Once we came back to class, he would ask, "Are you sufficiently frustrated?" We would reply with a collective, "Yes!" That's when he would smile and say, "Good, you're learning."

That's when I learned to put a high premium on frustration. Frustration can help you forge a path forward. It can push you past the common to the uncommon. Frustration can be the forerunner to discovery. If you're not frustrated, it's likely you're not learning. If you're not frustrated, you're probably sitting in a comfort zone that ultimately turns into a danger zone.

Let your frustration fuel you. Discontent can be the driver of new discoveries.

One of the ways frustration can fuel you is by pressing you to consider the ever-present opportunities for training that happen around you all the time. If you get frustrated with something that someone on your team does, rather than throwing up your hands in despair or venting about them in private, why not turn that frustration into a prayer that the Lord would open a strategic chance for you to speak truth and provide training for this person.

This is much like parenting. Anyone who has parented kids through adolescence knows that they are not always positioned to hear what they need to hear in order to make sense out of life. We can say the very same thing at two separate times and find two very differing responses. We might get frustrated with our kids for their rebellion or failure to listen. We can either react with scorn, or we can turn this frustration into a chance to speak words of grace and life to them. At times, God seems to open a unique door of receptivity in their hearts that allows us to share truth in a way that resonates.

The same is true for those on our team. We need to seek out the times when they are uniquely positioned to hear what we have to say. Often, this learning happens at the point of their own frustration. They get exasperated with a situation or circumstance and throw up their hands in despair. It's often in these moments that we can intersect their frustration with truth. However, this is usually only fruitful if we've been praying for God to give us the right opportunity to do so, and we've carefully considered what needs to be said.

How often do you provide spontaneous feedback on your team members' performance: never, rarely, frequently, or consistently?

If your answer is *never* or *rarely*, how is this affecting your team? What prevents you from providing more feedback?

If your answer is *frequently* or *consistently*, how is this impacting your team? What are you doing well in the way you provide feedback?

What do you need to change about how often you provide spontaneous feedback, or the way you provide spontaneous feedback?

Mark #6: Great Coaches Approach the Work as a Relationship Rather Than a Project

Let's play a game of word association. What word comes to mind when I say goal setting?

When I ask that question to a group of people, I get a variety of answers. *Excited, motivated, inspired.* Those are some of the positive responses. But I also get *frustrated, hesitant, fearful, apprehensive.*

Goal setting is an extremely valuable process for forward progress. However, each January when it's time for goal setting, many employees enter the process with fear and trepidation. Though most people would agree that the concept of goal setting is smart, the common application and expression of it is negative. Employees are told to write their goals and turn them in, but they never actually have a discussion with their supervisor about what they've written. They never receive encouragement or coaching around those goals, so the whole process feels like a box-ticking exercise rather than an active effort to help, based in the context of a loving relationship.

There are people out there who love goal setting because they have had a positive experience. They had a supervisor who worked with them to establish practical, relevant goals that were aligned with the mission of the organization as well as with the strengths of the individual. That supervisor then had regular conversations to help coach, encourage, and champion the leader toward progress of those goals.

One of the best ways to put goals in the context of a relationship is to connect the work to the person's overall sense of purpose and meaning in life. Why write a goal if the person has no desire to accomplish it, or if they don't feel gifted to pursue it? My guess is that 90 percent of the goals people write for their work are an exercise in futility rather than an expression of their passion.

One of the most important questions we can ask someone writing a goal is, "*Why* do you want to accomplish this goal?" At the top of each of my personal goals I answer that question.

For example, one of my goals is to create a new training tool that church leaders can use in staff meetings. My *why* is because pastors can struggle to use staff meeting time to help their staff continue to grow. Providing this tool will solve that problem, and it excites me to expand my development influence as the author of this type of tool.

Leading and goal setting in the context of a relationship would be much easier for us and those we lead if we follow a few simple rules:

Demonstrate a high confidence in your people. I've discovered the higher the confidence I have in people, the higher the confidence they have in themselves. When people have a high confidence in themselves, they're more likely to take greater risks and innovate in ways that add greater value to the ministry.

Praise progress not perfection. Imagine the difference it would make if leaders stopped looking for what people are doing wrong and started looking for what people are doing right—and then praised their progress. Team members would begin to discover and maximize their strengths. And that's always a win for an organization.

Establish shared expectations regarding performance outcomes. If you don't establish shared expectations, you'll experience shared frustrations. One of the wisest things you can do is talk to your people about what their performance will look like in the future, through goal setting, not just what it looked like in the past.

Give people the tools and resources they need to do their job well. Tools and resources will not only help your team be successful but also feel successful. Oftentimes it's not a lack of commitment or competency that creates poor performance; it's a lack of the right tools. And when you provide the tools they need, they will "feel" your support, and be encouraged.

Smile, laugh, and enjoy what you do. When you enjoy what you do, that joy spreads to the team. A simple smile is an expression that communicates that you love being there, and you love what you do. It's amazing how much smiling and humor can create a work culture people love. So, make sure you are enjoying meeting with your team members in a one-on-one coaching session. Lighten up, smile, laugh, let them know you enjoy being with them.

Lead from trust rather than from suspicion. If you lead from a position of suspicion, you create a tentative team. They will be guarded and operate out of fear. If you fail to establish a culture of trust, you've failed to establish a spirit of team.

Make it meaningful. Let's face it, sometimes the work our team does feels very menial. As a leader of a department, you know it all works together to make the mission move forward. But it can be easy for your team to forget. So make the work they do meaningful by always pointing them to the big-picture vision, celebrating the wins, and showing them that their contribution makes a difference.

Follow these rules, and your coaching will be much more relational, not just professional.

Which of the rules above reflects your strengths as a leader?

Which do you need to put into practice right away?

Conclusion

I hope this module will not only help you coach those you lead based on their performance goals, but also challenge you to set personal goals for your own life.

When I was a Dallas Seminary student, Dr. Howard Hendricks, who I mentioned earlier, had us write one-, five-, ten-, and twenty-year goals for our lives. It was a difficult assignment, but one of the most practical of my seminary career. I used that twelve-page document as a guide for my life for many years after I graduated seminary.

Hendricks told us, "Show me a person with a set of well-defined goals, and I'll show you a person on their way to achieving results."

Since that time, goal setting has been a consistent discipline in my life, not just for my work but for my personal life as well. Every December, I spend the month praying and processing what God wants to do in and through my life in the upcoming year.

While you may not use these exact questions, I encourage you to use these to help you process what God wants to do in your life in the next year.

- What one word do I want to characterize my life next year?
- What are three skills I need to grow in to accelerate my dream?
- Where do I need to grow in my character/walk with God?
- What habits/rhythms do I need to tweak or revive to achieve greater momentum?
- What do I need to stop doing?
- What do I need to do more of?
- What does God want me to focus on physically, spiritually, relationally, and vocationally over the next year?

Put It Into Practice

Choose one or more of the following to complete prior to meeting with your trainer.

1. Help a team member or a friend build a growth plan around a particular character trait or competency. Use the thirty-day personal growth template you learned about in module one. As they are working through their growth plan, schedule a time to meet with them to have a coaching conversation around the progress they are making. Be up front with them by letting them

know you are learning how to ask good coaching questions and will be practicing with them. Afterward, ask them what was helpful and what you could have done better.

2. Download the Goal Setting template at https://www.multiplygroup.org/goalsettingtemplate and fill it in, setting your own three to five performance goals. You can see a sample Goal Setting template at the end of this module. Share your performance goals with your trainer and ask for their feedback.

3. Practice using the Adaptive Leadership model. Ask a team member to set three to five goals and discuss their competence level for each goal. Then provide the appropriate level of direction (Guide, Coach, Champion) for each of those goals. After doing this for thirty to forty-five days, talk to your trainer about what you are doing well and what you could improve in relation to the Adaptive Leadership model.

4. Practice spontaneous coaching. Observe a team member in action and give them spontaneous feedback afterward. Discuss with your trainer what you did well, what you would do differently, and what you learned.

5. Observe a leader facilitating a coaching session, or ask someone who is a competent coach to do a coaching session with you. Interview the leader afterward to gain deeper insights into their methods and mindset as they coached the individual.

Reflect on Your Learning

Where did you grow the most in this competency?

What next step do you need to take to continue to grow in this competency?

Meet With Your Trainer

Consistent practice can be a great beginning to sharpening a skill, but developing a skill also requires processing what you learned with others. Meet with your trainer and discuss what you learned from this module.

Dig Deeper

If you are participating in an internship or want to continue to grow in the competency of coaching others, go to www.maclakeonline. com/internshiptools to download the companion guide to this book.

---

[1]   To discover how to structure your area of ministry, see my book *The Multiplication Effect: Building a Leadership Pipeline That Solves Your Leadership Shortage* (Nashville, TN: Thomas Nelson, 2020).

[2]   Ferdinand Fournies, *Why Employees Don't Do What They're Supposed to Do and What to do About It* (New York, NY: McGraw-Hill, 1999).

[3]   Ibid., vii–ix.

Sample Goal Setting Template

Setting up Your Goal Statement

What is it that you would like to accomplish?

Why is this goal important to the mission of your team/organization?

How will you go about accomplishing this goal?

When is your expected completion date for this goal?

Who will you involve in the execution and completion of this goal?

GOAL STATEMENT	Include the What, Why, Who, How, and When

I will recruit and train five new leaders to my team (what), in order to achieve a healthy one to five ratio, which will provide greater levels of care for my team members (why). I'll use the existing leaders on my team (who) to identify a list of twenty prospects and empower the existing leaders to have recruiting conversations (how), so that we can have these new leaders in place by September 6 (when).

SUCCESS INDICATORS	Key milestones that show progress

- Spend time praying about who to invite.
- Meet with my team to brainstorm a list of names we could potentially recruit.
- Meet with our communications team to develop a recruiting tool we can put in the hands of prospects.
- Read four articles (or videos) to develop my ability to recruit well.
- Make a list of twenty prospects.
- Enlist three of my existing leaders to help recruit the new leaders.
- Along with the three existing leaders, talk to five people each week over the next four weeks.

EXPECTED COMPLETION DATE	September 6

COMPETENCY LEVEL	☐ LEARNING ☑ GROWING ☐ MASTERING

Download a blank Goal Setting template at https://www.multiplygroup.org/goalsetting template.

6

Leading Meetings

Love them or hate them, it's rare to hold a neutral opinion about meetings. Most of our presuppositions about meetings are based on our past experience. If we've been a part of good, productive meetings, we are more likely to enjoy them and appreciate their value. If we've had a more negative experience, we tend to devalue them and dread leading or participating in meetings we deem to be a waste of time.

I've known some pastors who dislike meetings so much they decide not to have any at all. Other leaders think meetings are so vital that they have meetings for everything. Both approaches are overreactions that only reinforce people's negative opinions of meetings.

How we view meetings will determine how much we prepare, contribute, and engage in them. If a team member believes meetings are a waste of time, for example, they will likely not bring their best to team sessions.

When we mindlessly put meetings in people's calendars, we risk falling into routines that reinforce negative perceptions. We must therefore be intentional and strategic about how we use meeting times.

Very few leaders have been trained to lead a good meeting. They just do what they've observed others do. And many ministry leaders dislike meetings and feel guilty for scheduling them.

So instead of dreading meetings, why not get better at leading them?

While you cannot do anything about people's past experience of meetings, you can reshape their opinion by showing them how to lead a productive meeting.

Good meetings are an essential part of accomplishing your mission, as well as shaping your culture. Good meetings can

- intensify your team's commitment to the mission of your ministry;
- clarify the vision of your ministry;
- unify the members of your team;
- grow the character and competency of your team;
- identify obstacles and prioritize next steps; and
- increase the collaborative genius of your team.

When your team leaves one of your meetings, there should be a sense that their time was invested in achieving something beneficial to the mission of the ministry.

Accomplishing great things as a team doesn't just happen because people are working on a joint mission. Unity and productivity require team rhythms, and a big part of team rhythms includes meetings. In this session, you will learn six tips for leading productive meetings that people will value attending. As a result, you can create a highly productive team—a team that enjoys each other, respects each other, and even loves each other.

In this module we will consider the character trait of zeal and note how it contributes to planning and leading highly productive and unifying meetings.

First, let's work to define our terms:

Character: *Zeal*

Leaders demonstrate an enthusiastic commitment to that which God has called them to accomplish.

Competency: *Leading Meetings*

Plan and lead highly engaging meetings that enhance the team's productivity and unity.

Objectives

1. Assess your level of zeal.

2. Identify the traits of the team culture you want to build.

3. Plan a meeting using the 8 C template.

4. Observe and evaluate another leader facilitating a meeting.

5. Lead a portion or all of a meeting and receive feedback.

Deepen Your Character: *Zeal*

On more than one occasion I've looked at my friend Terence and said, "You are more like Jesus than anyone else I know." What strikes me most about Terence's life is the zeal he shows for the gospel. He will go to any lengths to demonstrate the love of Jesus.

It just so happens Terence's passion is for the homeless—those that are often overlooked in our society. There was a season in his life when he himself lived on the streets. Later on, he gave his life to Christ and, as he grew in his faith, so too did his desire to reach this overlooked sector of society. When he looks at this people group, his heart breaks because he is desperate for them to experience life in a different way, like he did. He is passionate for them to know and feel loved.

Terence demonstrates zeal in so many ways. But perhaps the most powerful example was when, in 2015, he moved out of his home for thirty days so that he could live under a bridge in downtown Atlanta, among the homeless. Kissing his wife and two small kids goodbye, he packed one change of clothes, a toothbrush, and a backpack. From November 25 to December 25, he lived on the streets. Every day he would interact with those who were homeless. He would listen to their stories and build relationships. He wasn't there to "save" them; he was there to connect, relate, and love them.

Terence is consumed by a zeal for the homeless to know the love of Jesus.

J. C. Ryle, in *Practical Religion* writes,

> Zeal in Christianity is a burning desire to please God, to do His will, and to advance His glory in the world in every possible way. It is a desire, which is not natural to men or women....
>
> This desire is so strong, when it really reigns in a person, that it impels them to make any sacrifice—to go through any trouble—to deny themselves anything—to suffer, to work, to labor, to toil, to spend themselves and be spent, and even to die—if only they can please God and honor Christ.
>
> A zealous person in Christianity is preeminently a person of one thing. It is not enough to say that they are earnest, strong, uncompromising, meticulous, wholehearted, and fervent in spirit. They only see one thing, they care for one thing, they live for one thing, they are swallowed up in one thing; and that one thing is to please God.[1]

Growing in zeal will help keep your life focused on that which is most important. It will keep you going when things get difficult. Zeal gives you courage, persistence, and focus. And yes, zeal is important in leading meetings as well.

Meetings should be anything but boring. When you meet with your team, you are discussing God's work! God's vision! And if we are zealous about God's work, it will carry over into our meetings. Yes, meetings sometimes require mundane elements, things that may not be exciting but still need to be communicated. But most of your meeting time should be used to share the vision God has put on your heart and to collaborate with your team to advance the next steps toward that vision. If that doesn't get you excited, I don't know what will.

I've personally sat in planning meetings with Terence, and although he is a quiet, mild-mannered guy, you feel the brokenness of his heart; you sense his zeal. You leave a meeting with Terence knowing that the time invested was time that will advance the kingdom mission God put on his heart.

Meeting with your team is the opportunity to plan actions that lead to God's ideal in your ministry. We must remember when we lead meetings, we are working on God's business, his priorities, the things he has placed on our heart. That's why my favorite part of meetings is when I get the chance to cast vision to my team or collaborate around a challenge in order to identify what God is saying to us. I'm not saying every meeting has to be led with expressive enthusiasm, but I am saying each meeting we lead should mean something in our spirit. Ask yourself, *how will the agenda items we talk about during this meeting advance the mission God has put on our hearts?* That's why it's so important we grow in this aspect of our character.

Scripture

In John 2, the disciples were struck by the zeal Jesus demonstrated when he drove the money changers from the temple. Jesus had come to demonstrate the love and grace of God, but the money changers had no interest in people's encounter with God. They just saw an opportunity to personally profit from the thousands of people pouring into Jerusalem to worship God during Passover. When Jesus saw what was taking place, he couldn't tolerate it and was moved to do something about it. He confronted the situation in a way that no one would forget.

As you read the following Scripture, meditate on what the author wishes to communicate, and answer the questions below. Allow the Holy Spirit to speak to you and challenge you as a leader about how you can develop your character so that you are filled with zeal in your own life and leadership.

John 2:13-17

When it was almost time for the Jewish Passover, Jesus went up to Jerusalem. In the temple courts he found people selling cattle, sheep and doves, and others sitting at tables exchanging money. So he made a whip out of cords, and drove all from the temple courts, both sheep and cattle; he scattered the coins of the money changers and overturned their tables. To those who sold doves he said, "Get these out of here! Stop turning my Father's house into a market!" His disciples remembered that it is written: "Zeal for your house will consume me."

Those selling animals for sacrifice and exchanging coins were providing a practical service for those who traveled great distances to come and make sacrifices at Passover. Why then was Jesus so disturbed by their actions?

What do you admire about Jesus' actions in this passage?

How has zeal been demonstrated in your life in the past thirty days?

What actions do you need to take to deepen zeal in your character?

Now that we have examined the character trait of zeal, we can begin to work through the core competency for this module: *Leading meetings—plan and lead highly engaging meetings that enhance the team's productivity and unity.* As you read what follows, note how zeal can undergird a leader's competency of leading meetings.

Develop Your Competency:
Leading Meetings
Preassessment

Before proceeding, complete the assessment below. In the final module of this training guide, you will retake it as a postassessment to measure your transformation and growth in this competency.

The following proficiencies demonstrate mastery of this module's competency. For each of them, give yourself a grade of A, B, C, D, or E to reflect your actual level of competency today. Giving yourself an A+ indicates you are a model for others to follow. An E indicates no mastery.

Proficiency	Preassessment
I plan meetings with a clear agenda that aligns with specific meeting objectives.	
I include frequent collaboration in meetings that draws out the creative thinking of the team and produces quality ideas.	
I finish meetings with clear next steps that are assigned to specific individuals.	
I share the objective(s) at the beginning of each meeting.	
I vary the focus of different meetings between development, collaborative problem solving, and strategic planning.	

Reflection Questions

How would you describe your level of experience in leading meetings?

What are your strengths and growth areas in leading meetings?

What is the most important thing you hope to learn from this session?

Leading Meetings

We just finished another meeting, and once again I walked out frustrated. *Why did we even meet?* I thought. *What did we accomplish? Did anyone leave with any action steps? Did we make any decisions, or did we just discuss items? Was this a waste of time?* And my biggest question: *What do I need to do to make our meetings better?*

Yes, you got that right. I was the one leading this ineffective meeting. You've probably been there too. You are bored or frustrated in the meetings that you have control of. That's doubly frustrating.

That's when I did a mental exercise that woke me up to my need to run better meetings. I wrote down the names of the seven people in my meeting. Next, I put each person's annual salary, which totaled around $420,000. Then I did the math and calculated that the meeting cost our church $202 for one hour. Since our meeting was a weekly occurrence, that meant our church was paying $10,100 each year for this team to meet. Yikes. So I began to ask, are we getting the bang for our buck out of these meetings? At that moment I realized I was wasting the church's money every time I lead unproductive meetings. And if you are not careful, bad meetings not only waste money, but they also waste the talent of your team. Well-run meetings capitalize on your team's strengths, insights, and experience in a way that helps you better accomplish the mission God has called you to.

As a leader of a ministry department, running meetings will be a regular part of your routine. Regardless of whether your role requires you to lead meetings with other staff or with volunteer leaders, it's essential you lead them well. If you are leading bad meetings, the signs will begin to show:

- People will make excuses to get out of the meeting.
- Team members will come unprepared.

■ People will attend the meeting but work on other things.

It only takes two or three unproductive meetings in a row to establish an unhealthy team culture. So let's consider six tips for running great meetings.

Tip #1: Use Meetings to Shape Team Culture

If you ask someone why meetings exist, you will likely hear, "To get things done," "To make decisions," or "To communicate information." While these are all true, there is an often-overlooked benefit to meetings: they can be used to shape team culture.

Meetings involve times when you are all together, thinking around the same topic, or tackling the same problem. A lot of informal discussion happens just before the meeting starts and right after a meeting ends. Inevitably someone says something funny, and everyone laughs together. Meetings allow your team to get to know each other. They teach your team to listen, work together, solve problems together, compromise, and discover each other's preferences and opinions. A study of 133 factory teams found that higher levels of interpersonal sensitivity, curiosity, and emotional stability resulted in more cohesive teams and increased prosocial behavior among team members.[2] This is why you should never just do a meeting to get it over with. You need to allocate time to engage in both the formal and informal benefits of a meeting.

Think through the type of team culture you desire to cultivate. For example, I want a team culture that is productive, relational, transparent, unified, and fun. Because I have defined those traits, I can now be intentional in leading meetings in ways that will shape this culture.

If I want a culture that is transparent, I might ask a question in a meeting like: "Okay, can someone give me three to four reasons why you think the solution we are discussing is not the best way to solve our problem?"

Or, because I want a culture where the team has fun, I might kick off our meeting with a question that gets people sharing and laughing.

Use your meetings to shape the culture of your team. We make a critical mistake when we just make meetings about the pragmatic elements of our work. Remember, people's personalities and behaviors are the avenue through which our values are ultimately expressed. If you want to shape your culture, you have to know and help shape the people on your team to express that culture.

Write down three to five words that describe the team culture you want to build?

What are some practical ways you will use meetings to shape that culture?

Tip #2: Predetermine the Objectives

The worst thing that can happen after investing sixty minutes of your life in a meeting is to walk out and say, "Wow, we just met and didn't accomplish a thing."

When considering meetings, the most important question you can ask is: "*Why* are we meeting?" For many, the answer is, "Because the meeting is on my calendar." If we are not careful, we fall into a meeting rut—meeting week after week without defining the objective(s) for meeting.

Think back to the last meeting you led or attended. What was the objective? How do you know? Simply look at the results of the meeting. If you spent the hour discussing and then choosing a new church management system, the objective could be stated as: Choose a new church management system we can start using by February.

If you brainstormed a list of potential volunteers for the upcoming Serve Day, the objective could have been verbalized this way: Identify twenty names of potential volunteers we can recruit to serve on the upcoming Serve Day.

But if you cannot point to specific results, then there were not specific objectives for that meeting. It's not uncommon to hear people leave a meeting saying, "We talked about a lot but didn't make any decisions." Or "We had some good discussion but didn't leave with any action steps." These types of meetings can be deceptive. You *feel* as if you are focusing on the right things, but none of it leads to any action.

To prevent this from happening, predetermine the objectives you would like to accomplish. You can do this by writing these objectives down. Much like goals, written objectives keep you on track for achieving what you set out to accomplish.

To help you process the objectives of your meetings, use action words. Here are a few I use frequently: *Define, Identify, Summarize, Complete, Solve, Teach, Articulate, Prioritize, Plan, Reframe, Design, Develop, Select, Choose, Determine, Modify, Evaluate, Train, Produce, Compile.*

Here are some examples:

- *Evaluate* the strengths and weaknesses of our assimilation process and *develop* a thirty-day plan for improvement.
- *Celebrate* the completion of the fall small group semester kickoff initiative, *identifying* five key lessons that can be carried forward for future efforts.

Once you have established the objective(s) for your meeting, then you should communicate that to people. You can email them ahead of time or at least tell them at the very beginning of the meeting what you plan to accomplish through the investment of their time. If people know the objectives and see those objectives achieved, then your meetings won't feel like a waste of time.

It's also important to ask yourself, *Does this need to be a meeting of a group of people, or can this be accomplished in a conversation with one person?* Sometimes we don't need to have a meeting; we just need to have a conversation. Again, if people see that you are intentionally planning not only the meeting objectives but the people who need to participate in order to accomplish those objectives, then they are much more likely to show up engaged when they are invited to participate, because they know that you've deemed them valuable to the meeting goals.

Tip #3: Select the Right Agenda

As a young pastor, I found myself stressing every time I had a meeting. I didn't want to waste people's time, so I would work hard and spend way too much time figuring out the perfect agenda. After a year of leading meetings, I realized the different meeting elements fell into a pattern. Once I identified the pattern, planning meetings became much easier. I discovered there are eight common elements I would use in meetings. I don't use all eight in one meeting! Typically, I will use three to five of the elements listed below in a single meeting.

I call these elements the 8 Cs. These elements help us answer the question: "How will we accomplish our objectives?" After writing your objectives, choose which elements will best accomplish them. Not only will this help you achieve your aims, but it will also keep the flow of the meetings from falling into a rut of the same pattern each time. Variety will create interest and maintain engagement.

Element #1—Connect. Teams often function as a group of individuals who are very siloed but come together to gain the necessary information, and then return to their silos to continue their work. Regularly take time to connect as people. Let your team get to know each other on a personal level.

This may be for as little as five minutes. You may want to use a question that will get them talking and warmed up. Questions like:

- What was the highlight of your weekend?
- What's something fun you've done with your kids recently?
- What is your favorite coffee shop in town and why?

The objective is just to connect relationally as a team and get to know each other better on a personal level. There are times when I keep this casual. Other times I make it more meaningful and personal. I may ask, "What has God shown you recently in his Word that you'd like to share with us?" Teams that know each other work better together.

Element #2—Celebrate. Visionary leaders are known for moving fast and then moving on to the next task. Sometimes we need to include time in our meetings to celebrate the achievements of the team or an individual. This doesn't have to take long. It can be as simple as, "What's something we can celebrate from our work over the past month?" This will help team members feel appreciated and give them a sense of accomplishment as the team celebrates what God has been doing in your work or ministry. Although this doesn't take much time, it can add great value. You're not looking for everyone to give an answer; you're just getting one or two people to respond, so you can genuinely celebrate some wins of how the team has seen God at work.

Element #3—Cast Vision. Vision is what keeps the fuel in the tank of the team. When they begin to lose sight of the vision, they lose the zeal to put their best into their work. So it's my role as a leader to cast vision in meetings. Sometimes it takes five minutes—just enough to give them an inspirational boost. Other times it's fifteen to thirty minutes to discuss deeper elements of the vision. When you keep the vision fresh, you fuel the zeal of your team.

Element #4—Check-Up. Leaders know we have to inspect what we expect. Meetings sometimes need to include a check-up on the progress of tasks or items that team members have committed to accomplish. These check-ups can often happen one-on-one outside meeting times, so they do not always need to be included in bigger meetings.

As I talk with different churches, one of the biggest challenges I hear them share is a lack of accountability. Accountability is partnering with an individual to provide consistent encouragement and challenge to achieve what they've committed to do. When you integrate occasional check-ups into meeting agendas, it will help raise the level of accountability among your team. It's likely impossible for you to check up on every detail, so you'll need to be selective to prioritize the most important check-ups for a meeting.

Element #5—Coach. A good leader can get the best out of a team member simply by getting them to use their strengths. But, as we explored in the previous module, great leaders go a step further. They not only challenge their people to use their strengths, but they also work with them to develop those strengths. Don't just use the talent of your people ... develop them.

I like to include leadership development at least once a month in team meetings. When you attempt to coach during a leadership meeting, you will find that it is helpful to take a large block of time so that you aren't rushed. Although you might be able to include multiple elements in a normal meeting, when you're coaching, you'll find you probably won't be able to do much more. The coaching portion of the agenda may last thirty to sixty minutes. The objective is to sharpen a leadership competency by learning from one another's experiences, as well as from any content you sent them to preview. During this segment of the meeting, you facilitate a discussion around an aspect of character or competency in which you want to see your team grow.

You can facilitate a robust development conversation with your team by watching a five- or ten-minute leadership video. At the end of the video, ask:

- What challenged you the most?
- What leadership strength did this affirm in you?
- What Scripture passage teaches or illustrates the primary concept of the video?
- What growth area did it reveal for you?
- What are the common mistakes leaders make in this area?
- What are some specific action steps you need to take to help you grow in this area?

Don't position yourself as the expert in the room; instead, let your team learn from one another. Make sure you end that time by having each person write down specific action steps they will take as a result of the training.[3]

Here are a few other ideas you can use when you want to add a leadership development segment to your meeting.

- Read a Scripture passage and let everyone share observations and discuss how it applies to their life and leadership. Conclude by asking everyone to identify a next step they will take.
- Send an article out and ask everyone to read it in advance. Discuss it together and ask everyone to identify the next steps they will take.
- Read a book together. Have them read one chapter or one section prior to the meeting. Discuss the chapter(s) together and identify next steps.
- Invite a field expert to attend your meeting—either in-person or via Zoom—and do a Q&A with them.

Element #6—Collaborate. There are times the team needs to work together to solve a problem, brainstorm best practices, or plan an event. This element tends to take twenty to forty minutes, depending on the objective. I try to work this element into my meetings at least every two weeks. Collaboration gets your team working together in ways that bring the best thinking of everyone on the team. If you want to build a sense of ownership among your team and see them maximize their strengths, collaboration is an essential element to include in your meeting agendas.

Element #7—Communicate. Communication is one of those items that doesn't have to take up much time in your meeting agenda, but it can reap a valuable payoff. If you don't communicate effectively, your team may not support some of the priority goals you're trying to move forward. So it's essential as a leader to help people know what they need to know.

The aim is to make sure everyone knows about any important upcoming events or dates. Ask everyone: *What are the important things coming up that we all need to be aware of?* Here you are simply making sure that everyone is on the same page by sharing the most important information that shapes the ministry moving forward.

Element #8—Care. A final element in good meetings is care. Here the aim is to pray for one another and share burdens. This is an easily overlooked element for some teams. Spend some time praying with and for each other. This allows your team to connect soul to soul and deepens their connection with each other.

Over the years, the 8 Cs have helped me plan well-balanced, intentional meetings. (I will be giving you a few sample agendas in Tip #4.) But an even bigger benefit is that this framework has taught my team how to lead meetings. Several years ago, I took on a new role with the North American Mission Board. There I led a team of eight to ten people. After a year of leading meetings with the team I told them that I was no longer going to lead all the meetings. It was their turn to start planning and leading all or portions of our team meetings. I turned this over to them because they had learned my 8 C meeting planning system, so I was confident they would do a great job of planning and leading our team meetings. I would delegate the meeting leadership to an individual on the team, ask them to run the agenda by me prior to the meeting, and then I would position myself in the meeting as a participant not the leader. It was such a joy to watch different team members take on leadership of our team. This was not only helpful to develop their competency of leading meetings, but it also built their confidence as leaders.

Which of the 8 Cs elements do you use most frequently in meetings you lead?

What is one way you could execute that element better?

Which of the elements do you tend to underutilize?

What difference could implementing this element more frequently make in your team?

Which element do you feel least equipped to utilize in meetings?

Tip #4: Select the Right Time Frame

As I was scheduling a meeting one day on my Google calendar, I noticed the default setting for a meeting is sixty minutes. Each time I would send a meeting invite to someone, it was automatically set for one hour, even though I may not need the full hour. It's important to schedule the right amount of time for a meeting. Even if we have a great meeting flow, if we spend four hours doing something we could accomplish in two, the meeting will feel like a waste of time.

Here are two sample agendas:

SAMPLE 1—45-Minute Meeting

Connect (10 minutes)—What was the highlight of your weekend?

Cast Vision (5 minutes)—Review the importance and progress of our one-year "battle cry" from our vision.

Collaborate (30 minutes)

- What is the best thing we do in the way we assimilate new people onto our ministry team?
- Where are we dropping the ball in the way we assimilate new people onto our ministry team?
- How is dropping that ball hurting us?
- Let's brainstorm some solutions.
- What action steps can we commit to right now?

SAMPLE 2—60-Minute Meeting

Celebrate (10 minutes)—What have you seen God do in your area of ministry over the past 30 days that we can celebrate together?

Coach (40 minutes)—Today, we are going to grow in the area of communication. We will watch a 10-minute video by Craig Groeschel on communication and then discuss the following questions.

- What stood out to you the most from this video?

- What are some common mistakes leaders make with communication?
- What Scripture passage teaches or illustrates the primary concept of the video?
- What strengths did this affirm in you?
- What growth area did it reveal for you?
- What next step do you need to take to grow in your communication skills?

Care (10 minutes)—How can we pray for one another?

You will notice these two sample agendas are very different from one another. My old way of leading meetings was to take the same agenda outline and just substitute the details under each header. Those meetings were boring and often lacked purpose.

But by using the 8 C template, you can plan highly engaging and purposeful meetings. Not every meeting will look or feel the same, and because your meetings aren't predictable, your team are more likely to stay engaged.

What stood out to you the most as you looked at the two meeting agenda samples?

Tip #5: Evaluate Your Meeting

Regular evaluation will help you avoid the common meeting mistakes. To evaluate, you can ask yourself these questions after every meeting.

- Did we accomplish the objective(s)?
- Did the team fully engage?
- Did everyone leave with clear action steps?
- If the answer is no to any of these, then ask a fourth question: What do we need to change?

It's important not to rush through this step. You may have an intuitive sense of what did or didn't work from a specific meeting, but you should take the time to jot down some notes shortly afterward. You'll be surprised at how quickly you will forget details. It might be helpful for you to also consult a trusted friend who was in the meeting to get their opinion. This will protect you from blind spots or distorted perceptions of what worked or what didn't.

Evaluate the meetings you lead:

What do you do well?

What could you do better?

How happy are you with your team's level of engagement in meetings?

How consistently does your team leave meetings with action steps they follow through on?

What could be improved to help follow through become more consistent?

Tip #6: Use Extended Meetings on Occasion to Accelerate Outcomes

Finally, think about using longer, more extended, meetings on occasion to focus on specific ministry objectives. Most meetings will be fairly short, and it might be difficult for you to focus on a certain topic for the time needed to consider it well.

These extended meetings might take the form of a quarterly half-day retreat or an annual planning session. This may look different based on the size, budget, and availability of leaders. It's vital that you consider who is best to invite to these meetings. There is nothing worse than blocking out an entire day and having the wrong people in the room to consider a big topic. Don't try to do too much in these settings. Find one primary focus, and spend the time you've allocated tackling this one, specific objective.

In 2007, I was leading a small church-planting organization. Our small team went to Breckenridge, Colorado for a team retreat. The two-day retreat was mainly structured around a series of questions I had laid out in advance. When I planned the agenda, I had no idea that the first question I asked would change everything for us. I asked, "What are the opportunities in front of us?" As we answered that question, we were amazed at how many responses we had. As we continued to discuss, we raised further questions, which eventually led us to clarity on who we were as an organization and where we were moving in the future. Within a year, the largest church-planting agency in the world acquired our organization and our church-planting system. Today, hundreds of church planters are assessed and trained through our system. It would've taken us decades to accomplish this. But that one question—"What are the opportunities in front of us?"—was a game changer.

What extended meetings do you currently use with your team?

How would you rate those on a scale of 1–5 (1 = low; 3 = average; 5 = a model for others to follow)?

What can you do to improve these meetings?

What type of extended meeting do you feel you need to add to your team's annual calendar?

Conclusion

Meetings get a bad rap. People love to poke fun at meetings and make them the butt of many jokes. But the truth is, you cannot lead toward your God-given mission without them. And I would go so far as to say, you cannot build a healthy team culture without them.

If you don't meet with your team, it will lead to poor communication, isolation, confusion, and disunity. Meetings that are not led well can lead to these same outcomes. It is therefore essential that you grow in zeal for the mission God has given you—and that you grow in the competency of leading meetings that yield highly productive teams.

Put It Into Practice

Choose one or more of the following to complete prior to meeting with your trainer.

1. Observe a meeting that someone else is leading, and write down the strengths and weaknesses of what you observed. Discuss what you learned from this observation experience with your trainer.

2. Write an agenda for an upcoming meeting, and send it to your trainer for review and feedback. Then lead the meeting, and invite your trainer to observe and give feedback.

3. Interview a leader who excels at leading effective and engaging meetings. Take notes, and identify two or three action steps you need to take in order to improve your own meetings. Share these with your trainer.

4. Identify a problem that needs to be solved, and plan a meeting with your team to get their input in solving the challenge. Plan specific questions you will ask in order to increase collaboration. Afterward, evaluate the level of engagement and collaboration among the team. How effective was the meeting in identifying solutions? How well did you listen?

Reflect on Your Learning

Where did you grow the most in this competency?

What next step do you need to take to continue to grow in this competency?

Meet With Your Trainer

Consistent practice can be a great beginning to sharpening a skill, but developing a skill also requires processing what you learned with others. Meet with your trainer and discuss what you learned from this module.

Dig Deeper

If you are participating in an internship or want to continue to grow in the competency of leading meetings, go to www.maclakeonline. com/internshiptools to download the companion guide to this book.

---

1   Taken from Erik Raymond, "What is Zeal?" *The Gospel Coalition*, August 26, 2014, www.thegospelcoalition.org/blogs/erik-raymond/what-is-zeal/.

2   Dave Winsborough and Tomas Chamorro-Premuzic, "Great Teams Are About Personalities, Not Just Skills," *Harvard Business Review*, January 25, 2017, https://hbr.org/2017/01/great-teams-are-about-personalities-not-just-skills.

3   See chapter four of Mac Lake, *Leading Leaders* (Cody, WY: 100 Movements Publishing, 2019) to learn how to create and lead huddles. Also, download free huddles from my website www.maclakeonline. com/huddles/.

7

Review Your Progress

Congratulations! Over the past few weeks and months, you have worked your way through six leadership modules, met with your trainer to debrief and discover new insights, and grown in your leadership character and competencies.

During this training, you have had a trainer walk alongside you serving as a model, providing feedback on your leadership, and giving you insights to grow in your character and competency. While it may feel like this journey is over, it is really just beginning.

Leadership is a lifelong learning process. And a big part of that process is doing periodic self-evaluation to discover your strengths, as well as the areas in which you need to continue to grow.

In this training guide, each module started by having you self-assess an aspect of your character. In each module, you also did a self-assessment, scoring yourself A–E on five proficiencies of each leadership competency. Altogether you evaluated your leadership on thirty proficiencies!

The final step of this training is a postassessment. You can do this on your own or with your trainer. This is a tool that you can come back to again and again as you continue to grow in your ability to lead leaders.

Postassessment: *Character*

Now that you have interacted with the content, it is time to reflect on what you have learned. This is the step where you must ask yourself, "How do I need to continue to grow in this aspect of my *character*?" Answer the following character questions and share your reflections during your meeting time with your trainer.

Module 1: *Self-Awareness*

Leaders are keenly aware and honest about how their emotional and behavioral tendencies impact those around them.

What was the biggest thing you learned about this aspect of your character?

In what way have you seen growth in this area?

What next step do you need to take to continue growing in this aspect of your character?

Module 2: *Self-Discipline*

Leaders yield to the Holy Spirit, making the right decisions despite their emotions and temptations.

What was the biggest thing you learned about this aspect of your character?

In what way have you seen growth in this area?

What next step do you need to take to continue growing in this aspect of your character?

Module 3: *Discernment*

Leaders recognize and respond to the presence and activity of God.

What was the biggest thing you learned about this aspect of your character?

In what way have you seen growth in this area?

What next step do you need to take to continue growing in this aspect of your character?

Module 4: *Authenticity*

Leaders acknowledge they are broken and imperfect while trusting God's grace and his Spirit to conform them to the image of Christ.

What was the biggest thing you learned about this aspect of your character?

In what way have you seen growth in this area?

What next step do you need to take to continue growing in this aspect of your character?

Module 5: *Genuine Love*

Leaders respond in a patient, caring, and honest manner to those with whom they interact.

What was the biggest thing you learned about this aspect of your character?

In what way have you seen growth in this area?

What next step do you need to take to continue growing in this aspect of your character?

Module 6: *Zeal*

Leaders demonstrate an enthusiastic commitment to that which God has called them to accomplish.

What was the biggest thing you learned about this aspect of your character?

In what way have you seen growth in this area?

What next step do you need to take to continue growing in this aspect of your character?

Postassessment:
Competency

Now that you have interacted with the content and put it into practice, it is time to reflect on what you have learned. This is the step where you must ask yourself, "How do I need to continue to grow in this aspect of my *competency*?" Fill your preassessment results in the following tables and then score yourself again according to the degree of growth you feel you've experienced. (For example, you might have scored yourself a C in preassessment and a B in postassessment.) Giving yourself an A+ indicates you are a model for others to follow. An E indicates no mastery. Then answer the questions and share your reflections during your meeting time with your trainer.

Module 1: *Personal Development*

Continuously pursue learning opportunities to gain new insights and wisdom that enable growth in character and leadership competencies.

Where did you grow the most in this competency?

What next step do you need to take to continue to grow in this competency?

Proficiency	Preassess-ment	Postassess-ment	Notes
I can easily articulate areas of growth God desires in my character or competency.			
I can demonstrate a high degree of intentionality with personal development plans.			
I use a system to maximize learning retention.			
I regularly learn from high-capacity leaders.			
I leverage the benefits of accountability for personal development.			

Module 2: *Time Management*

Steward time in a wise manner that minimizes distractions and maximizes personal contribution to the organization's mission.

Where did you grow the most in this competency?

What next step do you need to take to continue to grow in this competency?

Proficiency	Preassess-ment	Postassess-ment	Notes
I make decisions on how to use time, based on personal strengths and mission.			
I consistently prioritize assignments from most important to least important.			
I routinely block out how time will be used on the calendar.			
I say "no" to non-essential tasks or opportunities that do not align with priorities.			
I intentionally block out distractions in order to stay focused on priority assignments.			

Module 3: *Making Decisions*

Weigh a variety of options to make a prayerful, wise choice that reflects God's desired outcome.

Where did you grow the most in this competency?

What next step do you need to take to continue to grow in this competency?

Proficiency	Preassessment	Postassessment	Notes
I ground all my decisions in prayer and God's Word.			
I give appropriate consideration to others' advice and wisdom in decision making.			
I seek out as much information as possible and make decisions in light of the appropriate information.			
I understand how the past, present, and future can influence decisions.			
I display courage to make wise decisions even when it may not be the popular thing to do.			

Module 4: *Communication*

Communicate clearly so others understand and take the appropriate action.

Where did you grow the most in this competency?

What next step do you need to take to continue to grow in this competency?

Proficiency	Preassess-ment	Postassess-ment	Notes
I consistently display a positive attitude when communicating.			
I ask questions and listen in order to ensure communication has been clear.			
I help team members understand and appreciate my personality and communication style.			
I strive to bring clarity to team members regarding the big picture, as well as details they need to be aware of to do their job.			
I demonstrate a willingness to take responsibility and apologize when appropriate.			

Module 5: *Coaching Others*

Guide an individual through a thought process to discover insights and action steps that lead to further development in their life and leadership.

Where did you grow the most in this competency?

What next step do you need to take to continue to grow in this competency?

Proficiency	Preassess- ment	Postassess- ment	Notes
I see the strengths and potential of others.			
I prefer to use thought-provoking questions over simply giving advice.			
I capitalize on team members' failures and successes in order to maximize development.			
I give challenging assignments that help individuals grow.			
I observe team members in action and provide them with honest, constructive feedback.			

Module 6: *Leading Meetings*

Plan and lead highly engaging meetings that enhance the team's productivity and unity.

Where did you grow the most in this competency?

What next step do you need to take to continue to grow in this competency?

Proficiency	Preassessment	Postassessment	Notes
I plan meetings with a clear agenda that aligns with specific meeting objectives.			
I include frequent collaboration in meetings that draws out the creative thinking of the team and produces quality ideas.			
I finish meetings with clear next steps that are assigned to specific individuals.			
I share the objective(s) at the beginning of each meeting.			
I vary the focus of different meetings between development, collaborative problem solving, and strategic planning.			

For the Trainer

As a leader yourself, you have much wisdom and insight to offer those who are in the process of becoming leaders too. The *Leading a Department* training is designed to help these individuals gain the knowledge and experience they need to lead effectively.

As a trainer, you are both a model and a mentor. As a model, you allow those you are training to watch you demonstrate both the character and competency each module covers. You are the best curriculum others can read.

As a mentor, you observe and give trainees feedback, as they put what they're learning into practice. Approach your time together in the spirit of a fellow learner rather than the spirit of an instructor. The mentoring component is accomplished better by training two to three people at one time than going through it one-on-one. When you have two or three, you'll have better discussions, and the participants will learn from one another as well.

Tips

Schedule

Before meeting with your trainees, create a proposed schedule of when and where you will meet. A biweekly rhythm should give them plenty of time to read the module and do the assignments. Remember, however, that the purpose is transformation—growth in the character and competency of those you are training—so do not rush modules. Feel free to meet two or even three times for one module if you feel that's necessary. One of the beauties of this approach to training is you can have a flexible timeline.

Model

Modeling is one of the most effective means of training others. Invite the trainee to observe you in your leadership role so that you can model these particular competencies. For example, if you are facilitating discussion in your group or in a team meeting, ask your trainees to come and observe. After they have observed you, ask them what they learned from watching you in action.

Meet

When you meet with those you are training, I recommend you schedule fifty to seventy-five minutes. Each module has more content than you can cover in that amount of time, so preview the questions and mark those that will bring out the most learning. Don't feel like you have to cover every single question, and feel free to ask follow-up questions to increase learning. But also don't jump back and forth within the module, because the content is arranged in an order that delivers maximum insight and practical learning. What follows is a general guide to a training meeting. Remember to be flexible and allow the Holy Spirit to use you to help each learner truly grasp and learn what God has for them in each module. A typical training session looks something like the following.

1. Connect (5–10 minutes)
Spend the first few minutes allowing the group to connect relationally and catch up on what's been going on in their week. Avoid just rushing into the content. Remember, this is a relational approach to development, which means allowing people time to get to know each other well.

2. Celebrate (5 minutes)

Ask, "What is something we've seen God do since the last time we met that we can celebrate?" You don't have to spend a lot of time on this, but take a few minutes and enjoy the work God is doing in your trainees' lives or ministries. This celebration time can reveal some important things in the lives of these leaders and can strengthen their faith as they watch how God is working in one another's lives.

3. Coach (30–45 minutes)

Walk through the questions and assessments. The trainee should have worked through all the content of the module before you meet with them, so you are asking them to discuss matters they have already considered and reflected on personally. The material provided is more than enough for a forty-five-minute discussion. Make sure you are prepared to discuss what is most relevant for your particular learners. (See "Facilitate" and "Assign" below.)

4. Communicate (1–2 minutes)

Ask, "What important upcoming events do we all need to be aware of?" You won't need to spend much more than one minute on this. But it is important to communicate any key events coming up at the church, as well as the details for your next training session.

5. Care (10–15 minutes)

Make sure you save time to ask, "How can we pray for each other?" Spend a few minutes praying with and for each other. While this is a general guide, remember to be flexible and allow the Holy Spirit to use you to help each learner truly grasp and learn what God has for them in each module.

Facilitate

Remember that as a trainer, you are a facilitator of discussion. It is important to get your trainees talking about what they learned. The temptation will be to talk too much and tell them everything you know about each of the topics. Although your experience and insights are important, it is just as important that your learners verbalize what they are learning. Utilize the questions to guide them to share what they are discovering, then share your insights as a supplement to their learning experience. In addition, I always tell my trainers, "The questions in the modules stimulate thought and provide good answers, but your follow-up questions are where your learners will find the gold." I recommend using the Five Hats to stimulate a deeper level of thinking. For example, let's say you asked, "Would you say you are good at making decisions?" And the trainee replied, "Sometimes I think I'm good at making decisions, but then other people on my team don't always seem as enthusiastic about the choices I've made." Here are five options for how you might follow up on that answer.

1. Fisherman: Point of View Question
Ask for the person's perspective or point of view in order to discover opportunity or obstacles. From the example above I might ask, "Why do you think you're good at making decisions?"

2. Reporter: Story Question
Draw out a story from the person's past experience on the topic in order to discover a leadership insight. I might ask, "You said your team sometimes don't seem enthusiastic about your decisions. Can you talk us through an example of when this has happened?"

3. Physician: Self-Assessment Question

Ask the individual to diagnose themselves in order to discover their strengths or weaknesses. I might ask, "On a scale of 1–5, with 5 being high, how would you describe your skill level in decision making? Why did you choose [insert number they chose]? What do you need to do to grow to a [insert one number higher than they chose]?"

4. Contractor: List Building Question

Ask the individual or group to identify a list or framework to discover different perspectives or insights. I might ask, "What are four reasons that can cause someone to struggle to make a decision?"

5. Pilot: Action Step Question

After a member has identified something to work on, ask the individual to identify a flight path—practical next steps that will guide them in the direction of growth and development. I might ask, "What three action steps could you take that will help you ensure your team are on board with a decision you make?"

Assign

While each module provides "Put It Into Practice" assignments, feel free to change those to give them assignments that fit the particular ministry role they are being trained for.

Module Questions

All the questions from the modules have been organized in a simple way on the following pages so you can seamlessly flow through the training questions to help those you are training learn from what they've read and put into practice.

Module 1: Self-Awareness

In this module, we will focus on the character trait of self-awareness and the competency of personal development, and explore how these work together to help you grow.

Deepen Your Character: Self-Awareness

Let's begin by focusing on the character portion of this study. In this module, the focus is on **Self-Awareness—**_Leaders are keenly aware and honest about how their emotional and behavioral tendencies impact those around them._

(Read Psalm 139:23–24 together.)

Psalm 139:23–24

Search me, God, and know my heart;
test me and know my anxious thoughts.
See if there is any offensive way in me,
and lead me in the way everlasting.

In this psalm David reflects on four characteristics of God:

- Omniscient—he has perfect knowledge (1–6).
- Omnipresent—he is everywhere, not limited by time or space (7–12).
- Omnipotent—he is all powerful (13–18).
- Holy—he is without sin, perfect in every way (19–24).

As David reflected on God's character, it led him to a moment of self-examination where he said, "Search me, God, and know my heart; test me and know my anxious thoughts. See if there is any offensive way in me, and lead me in the way everlasting" (23–24).

- Which aspect of God's character in this psalm do you need to become more aware of? Why?
- How would you assess your level of self-awareness: low, medium, or high? Explain the reasoning for your answer.
- It is difficult to assess your level of self-awareness on your own. Who can you invite to give you feedback on your self-awareness?
- If God were to point out an "offensive way" in your life right now, what do you think he would focus on?
- What action steps can you take to grow in self-awareness?

Develop Your Competency: *Personal Development*

Now that we've talked about how we can grow in self-awareness, let's talk through what you learned about the competency: **Personal Development**—*Continuously pursue learning opportunities to gain new insights and wisdom that enable growth in character and leadership competencies.*

How did you answer the following questions in the preassessment?

- What barriers to consistent personal development do you most commonly face?
- Pick one barrier and write below three ways you can eliminate that barrier.
- What do you hope to gain from this session?

Personal Development Efforts Chart

- How would you evaluate the intentionality of your development time on a scale of 1–5: 1 – I am not intentional, 3 – I am somewhat intentional, 5 – I am highly intentional?
- What would you change to make that development time more deliberate?

Areas in Which You'd Like to Grow: Character and Competencies Table

- What would you add to each list in the table?
- What one growth area would you like to start with first?

Stop Reading Books

- Which of the tips from this section is most helpful to you? Why?
- How will you apply this section this week?

Get Around Big Leaders

- List the names of three big leaders you would like to learn from.
- What are three questions you would ask if you had the opportunity to meet one of them?

Put It Into Practice

Developing a new skill requires practice. Discuss with those you are training what they learned about personal development from their "Put It Into Practice" assignments.

1. Create a list of character traits and competencies in which you would like to grow. Build on the list provided in this module. File your list somewhere you can access it readily when it's time to build a new growth plan.

2. Use the template provided in this module to build a thirty-day personal development plan. Identify an accountability partner who can help you stick with the plan. Or purchase the Personal Growth Plan Workbook to access thirty-two competency growth plans. You can find these at www.multiplygroup.org.

3. Reach out to a "big leader" and ask them for thirty to sixty minutes of their time, so you can ask them questions. Make a list of ten questions prior to meeting with them. Take a pen and notebook so you can record their answers. Share what you learned with your trainer.

4. Practice the advice from this module on reading books. Share with your trainer how this system of reading helped you retain and learn more.

5. Interview two to three people who lead the ministry department you lead or desire to lead. From these interviews create a list of five essential competencies for leading your specific ministry department. Share these with your trainer.

Reflect on Your Learning

- Where did you grow the most in this competency?
- What next step do you need to take to continue to grow in this competency?

Module 2: Time Management

In this module, we will focus on the character trait of self-discipline and the principles and techniques that will maximize your time management.

Deepen Your Character: *Self-Discipline*

Let's begin by focusing on the character portion of this study. In this module, the focus is on **Self-Discipline** — *Leaders yield to the Holy Spirit, making the right decisions despite their emotions and temptations.*

(Read 1 Corinthians 9:24–27 together.)

1 Corinthians 9:24–27

Do you not know that in a race all the runners run, but only one gets the prize? Run in such a way as to get the prize. Everyone who competes in the games goes into strict training. They do it to get a crown that will not last, but we do it to get a crown that will last forever. Therefore I do not run like someone running aimlessly; I do not fight like a boxer beating the air. No, I strike a blow to my body and make it my slave so that after I have preached to others, I myself will not be disqualified for the prize.

- Paul says he runs in a way to get the prize. He disciplines himself so he will not be disqualified from the prize. What do you think the "prize" was for Paul? What is the prize for you? (Be as specific as possible.)
- What does "strict training" look like in your life?
- Think of an area in which you need to be more self-disciplined?

Why do you struggle in this particular area? In what way does or could this area of struggle hurt your credibility as a leader of a ministry? What are two or three things you can do this week to demonstrate more self-discipline in this area?

Develop Your Competency: *Time Management*

Now that we have examined the character trait of self-discipline, let's talk through what you learned about the competency: **Time Management**—*Steward time in a wise manner that minimizes distractions and maximizes personal contribution to the organization's mission.*

How did you answer the following questions in the preassessment?

- Which of the proficiencies listed reflect your top time-management strength?
- Which one reflects your top time-management growth area?
- What do you hope to gain from this session?

Stay on Mission

- How would you describe your life mission in one sentence?
- How well did you align your activities last week with that mission?

Prioritize the Right Things

- Which of the following areas are you doing best with? Which do you need to do better?
  - Taking care of myself physically
  - Protecting my marriage
  - Involving my family
  - Pursuing silence and solitude

- What practical step can you take over the next thirty days to do better in the area you need to improve?
- How often have you intentionally scheduled solitude into your calendar over the past thirty days?
- Think back to your last day off. Were you able to completely disconnect, or were you still preoccupied with work? If you were preoccupied with work, why?
- What do you need to implement in order to protect yourself from working too much?

Know Yourself

- What three words describe your strengths?
- If you were to write a job description for yourself, what would it include?
- What are your top three responsibilities?
- What are you good at, and does it align with what you are responsible for? If the answer is "no," what do you need to change?

Grow Your Ability to Focus

- What are the biggest distractions you typically face? Make a list of your top three.
- What can you do to defend yourself against those?

Put It Into Practice

Developing a new skill requires practice. Discuss with those you are training what they learned about time management from their "Put It Into Practice" assignments.

1. Research how to write a life mission statement. Write a one-sentence mission statement and present it to those who know you best to get their feedback. Share what you learned with your trainer.

2. Meet with someone who leads the area of ministry you lead or aspire to lead. Ask them the following questions, and discuss what you learned afterward with your trainer.
   a. How do you prepare for your week?
   b. What is the biggest time management challenge in your area of ministry?
   c. What things are most important to delegate to others in this area of ministry?
   d. How do you deal with people in your ministry who habitually waste your time?
   e. What advice do you have for me about managing my time?

3. Practice time blocking by blocking out your 9–5 for the upcoming week. Put meetings, tasks, and projects in sixty- to ninety-minute

blocks on your calendar. Review this with your trainer at the beginning of the week. Then evaluate it with your trainer at the end of the week.

4. Keep a time log of how you spend your time for a full week. Include your times of solitude and sabbath so you can evaluate not just how you are spending your work time, but how well you are practicing silence and solitude. Journal what you learned from the experience.

5. Practice identifying your three WINs for each day. Do this for a full week, and discuss with your trainer what you learned from this experience.

Reflect on Your Learning

- Where did you grow the most in this competency?
- What next step do you need to take to continue to grow in this competency?

Module 3: Decision Making

In this module, we will focus on deepening your discernment and developing your competency of making decisions.

Deepen Your Character:
Discernment

Let's begin by focusing on the character portion of this study. In this module, the focus is on **Discernment**—*Leaders recognize and respond to the presence and activity of God.*

(Read Romans 12:2 together.)

Romans 12:2

Do not conform any longer to the pattern of this world, but be transformed by the renewing of your mind. Then you will be able to test and approve what God's will is—his good, pleasing and perfect will.

- What "patterns of this world" do leaders tend to conform to the most?
- Which one is the biggest challenge for you?
- How would you describe the process of being transformed?
- In what area of your life or leadership do you need God to give you greater discernment in right now? In what ways can you "test and approve" his will?

Develop Your Competency:
Making Decisions

Now that we have examined the character trait of discernment, let's talk through what you learned about the competency:

Making Decisions— *Weigh a variety of options to make a prayerful, wise choice that reflects God's desired outcome.*

How did you answer the following questions in the preassessment?

- What's the most difficult decision you've had to make as a leader?
- What did you do well in the way you processed and made that decision?
- What would you do differently?
- In which of the proficiencies listed do you need to grow the most?

Four Reasons We Get Stuck in Decision Making

- Which of the reasons do you typically struggle with the most?
- How has that hurt your leadership in the past?

Two Big Decisions (written at the beginning of the module)

- What are you not acting on that you need to act on?
- What's holding you back?
- What do you need to do this week in order to move that decision forward?

Decisions That Fit Our Values

- Write a list of the personal values you have for your life.

- Next, process a personal decision you are wrestling with, using your values.
- How did filtering a decision through your values help bring clarity to the decision?

Am I Really the One Who Should Be Making This Decision?

- What decisions do you need to stop making? Who will you give the decision-making responsibility to?

Put It Into Practice

Developing a new skill requires practice. Discuss with those you are training what they learned about decision making from their "Put It Into Practice" assignments.

1. Think about the toughest decision facing you right now, and spend time praying for wisdom and discernment before making the decision. Seek out specific Scriptures that might relate to that decision. Write a list of options, considering the potential benefits and consequences of each option. Ask the Lord, "What is the wise thing to do?" Then commit to doing it.

2. Create a step-by-step decision-making process you can use in the future to help you make informed, well-thought-out decisions.

3. Interview a church staff member about his or her decision-making process. What did you learn? What action steps are you going to incorporate into your own life? Meet with your trainer and share what you learned.

4. Seek advice from two or three people regarding a decision you're facing. What did you learn? How well did you listen? Was the advice helpful?

5. Delegate a decision to someone on your team. Tell them why you chose them and give them the authority and support they need to make the decision. Debrief this with your trainer, and discuss what you learned by delegating a decision.

Reflect on Your Learning

- Where did you grow the most in this competency?
- What next step do you need to take to continue to grow in this competency?

Module 4: Communication

In this module, we will focus on growing in authenticity and learning the fundamental principles for becoming an effective communicator.

 Deepen Your Character: *Authenticity*

Let's begin by focusing on the character portion of this study. In this module, the focus is on **Authenticity—** *Leaders acknowledge they are broken and imperfect while trusting God's grace and his Spirit to conform them to the image of Christ.*

(Read 1 Corinthians 2:1–5 together.)

1 Corinthians 2:1–5

And so it was with me, brothers and sisters. When I came to you, I did not come with eloquence or human wisdom as I proclaimed to you the testimony about God. For I resolved to know nothing while I was with you except Jesus Christ and him crucified. I came to you in weakness with great fear and trembling. My message and my preaching were not with wise and persuasive words, but with a demonstration of the Spirit's power, so that your faith might not rest on human wisdom, but on God's power.

- What do you learn about authenticity from Paul's example?
- Who is the most authentic leader you know? What would you like to emulate from their life?
- In what area of your life do you find yourself most tempted to "manage your image"? How do you typically do that? What next step do you need to take to be more authentic in that aspect of your life?

Develop Your Competency: *Communication*

Now that we have examined the character trait of authenticity, let's talk through what you learned about the competency: **Communication—***Communicate clearly so others understand and take the appropriate action.*

How did you answer the following questions in the preassessment?

- How do you think your family would rate your communication on a scale of 1–5, with 1 being low, 5 being exceptionally high? How about your team? Co-workers? Boss?
- Where do you need to grow in your communication skills?

Learn to Be Likeable

- In which of the five tips given are you strongest? How do you see that strength enhancing your ability to communicate with others, particularly your team?
- In which do you most need to grow? How do you see that growth area hindering your ability to communicate with others, particularly your team?
- What can you do this week to grow your likeability factor?

Help Your Team Understand Who You Are

- Think back to a time you were on-boarded to a new team? What do you wish the leader had done differently that would have helped you better acclimatize?
- Imagine you just recruited a new leader into your area of

ministry. What are four to five things you would want them to know about you?

Listen More Than You Talk

- What stood out to you the most from this segment?
- What makes listening a challenge for you?
- Who do you need to listen to more closely? What impact might increased listening have in that relationship?

Strive For Clarity

- What did you discover about your communication skills in this segment?

Be Quick to Apologize

- Is it easy or difficult for you to give a sincere apology? If it's difficult for you, how has that impacted your leadership?
- Is there anyone you need to apologize to right now? What is holding you back? What next step do you need to take?

Put It Into Practice

Developing a new skill requires practice. Discuss with those you are training what they learned about communication from their "Put It Into Practice" assignments.

1. Interview someone who leads the area of ministry you currently lead or are preparing to lead. Ask them the following questions about communication:

    a.   What are the common practices you use to maintain healthy communication with your team?

    b.   Most of the people we work with are volunteers. What challenges do you face in keeping your team of volunteers informed?

    c.   What tools, apps, resources, or rhythms do you use to help communicate well with your team?

    d.   What is the biggest piece of advice you would give me about communicating with my team?

2. Observe someone who leads the same area of ministry you lead or will be leading. Ask to follow them in a situation where they are interacting and communicating with their team. Write down what you learn from seeing them in action.

3. Delegate a project or task to a team member, and ask your trainer or someone else to observe your communication and give you feedback.

4. Invite an acquaintance, team member, or potential team member for coffee to get to know them better. Practice asking questions and being a good listener. Share what you learned from this intentional listening exercise with your trainer.

Reflect on Your Learning

- Where did you grow the most in this competency?
- What next step do you need to take to continue to grow in this competency?

Module 5: Coaching Performance

In this module, we will focus on growing in genuine love and learning the fundamental principles for becoming an effective coach.

 Deepen Your Character: *Genuine Love*

Let's begin by focusing on the character portion of this study. In this module, the focus is on **Genuine Love—** *Leaders respond in a patient, caring, and honest manner to those with whom they interact.*

(Read 1 Corinthians 13:4–8 together.)

1 Corinthians 13:4–8

Love is patient, love is kind. It does not envy, it does not boast, it is not proud. It does not dishonor others, it is not self-seeking, it is not easily angered, it keeps no record of wrongs. Love does not delight in evil but rejoices with the truth. It always protects, always trusts, always hopes, always perseveres. Love never fails.

- Which aspect of love in this passage do you most easily display?
- Which is a challenge for you?
- Think of a team member, family member, or co-worker you may currently be frustrated with. What can you do this week to express genuine love to this individual?

 Develop Your Competency: *Coaching Others*

Now that we have examined the character trait of genuine love, let's talk through what you learned about the competency:

Coaching Others—*Guide an individual through a thought process to discover insights and action steps that lead to further development in their life and leadership.*

How did you answer the following questions in the preassessment?

- Who has been the best life or leadership coach you've ever had? What made them a good coach?
- If you've never had a leadership coach, what do you feel like you have missed out on?
- In what three ways do you feel you need to grow in your coaching ability?

Great Coaches Listen and Ask Effective Questions

- On a scale of 1–5 (1 = low; 3 = average; 5 = a model for others to follow), how would you rank your ability to ask coaching questions?
- What do you do well as a coach?
- In what specific ways do you need to improve in asking coaching questions?

Great Coaches Agree on Performance Goals in Advance

- How do you feel about using performance goals in your work? Why do you feel this way?
- If you had a team member question the value of setting performance goals, what would you tell them?
- What is your level of experience in coaching others based on the goals they set: No experience, little experience, or high experience?

Great Coaches Discuss and Agree on the Type of Input They Will Provide

- What was most helpful to you from this section?
- What is your default approach: Guide, Coach, or Champion? How could learning to use the other two approaches improve your leadership?
- What next step do you need to take to grow in the other two approaches of Adaptive Leadership?

Great Coaches Take Advantage of Spontaneous Development Opportunities

- How often do you provide spontaneous feedback on your team members' performance: never, rarely, frequently, or consistently?
- If your answer is *never* or *rarely*, how is this affecting your team? Why are you not providing more feedback?
- If your answer is *frequently* or *consistently*, how is this impacting your team? What are you doing well in the way you provide feedback?
- What do you need to change about how often you provide spontaneous feedback, or the way you provide spontaneous feedback?

Great Coaches Approach the Work as a Relationship Rather Than a Project

- Which of the rules in this section reflects your strengths as a leader?
- Which do you need to put into practice right away?

Put It Into Practice

Developing a new skill requires practice. Discuss with those you are training what they learned about coaching performance from their "Put It Into Practice" assignments.

1. Help a team member or a friend build a growth plan around a specific aspect of character or competency. Use the personal growth template you learned about in module one. As they are working through their growth plan, schedule a time to meet with them to have a coaching conversation around the progress they are making. Be up front with them by letting them know you are learning how to ask good coaching questions and will be practicing with them. Afterward, ask them what was helpful and what you could have done better.

2. Download the Goal Setting template at https://www.multiplygroup. org/goalsettingtemplate and fill it in, setting your own three to five performance goals. Share your performance goals with your trainer and ask for their feedback.

3. Practice using the Adaptive Leadership model. Ask a team member to set three to five goals, and discuss their competence level for each goal. Then provide the appropriate level of direction (Guide, Coach, Champion) for each of those goals. After doing this for thirty to forty-five days, talk to your trainer about what you are doing well and what you could do better when using the Adaptive Leadership model.

4. Practice spontaneous coaching. Observe a team member in action and give them spontaneous feedback afterward. Ask your trainer to observe you providing the feedback if possible. If not, discuss with

your trainer what you did well, what you would do differently, and what you learned.

5. Observe a leader facilitating a coaching session, or ask someone who is a competent coach to do a coaching session with you. Interview the leader afterward to gain deeper insights into their methods and mindset as they coached the individual.

Reflect on Your Learning

- Where did you grow the most in this competency?
- What next step do you need to take to continue to grow in this competency?

Module 6: Leading Meetings

In this module, we will focus on the character trait of zeal and note how it contributes to planning and leading highly productive and unifying meetings.

Deepen Your Character: *Zeal*

Let's begin by focusing on the character portion of this study. In this module, the focus is on **Zeal**—*Leaders demonstrate an enthusiastic commitment to that which God has called them to accomplish.*

(Read John 2:13–17 together.)

John 2:13–17

When it was almost time for the Jewish Passover, Jesus went up to Jerusalem. In the temple courts he found people selling cattle, sheep and doves, and others sitting at tables exchanging money. So he made a whip out of cords, and drove all from the temple courts, both sheep and cattle; he scattered the coins of the money changers and overturned their tables. To those who sold doves he said, "Get these out of here! Stop turning my Father's house into a market!" His disciples remembered that it is written: "Zeal for your house will consume me."

- Those selling animals for sacrifice and exchanging coins were providing a practical service for those who traveled great distances to come and make sacrifices at Passover. Why then was Jesus so disturbed by their actions?
- What do you admire about Jesus' actions in this passage?

- How has zeal been demonstrated in your life in the past thirty days?
- What actions do you need to take to deepen zeal in your character?

Develop Your Competency: *Leading Meetings*

Now that we have examined the character trait of zeal, let's talk through what you learned about the competency: **Leading Meetings**—*Plan and lead highly engaging meetings that enhance the team's productivity and unity.*

How did you answer the following questions in the preassessment?

- How would you describe your level of experience in leading meetings?
- What are your strengths and growth areas in leading meetings?
- What was the most important thing you hoped to learn from this session?

Tip #1: Use Meetings to Shape Team Culture

- Write down three to five words that describe the team culture you want to build?
- What are some practical ways you will use meetings to shape that culture?

Tip #3: Select the Right Agenda

- Which of the 8 Cs elements do you use most frequently in meetings you lead?
- What is one way you could execute that element better?
- Which of the elements do you tend to underutilize?
- What difference could implementing this element more frequently make in your team?
- Which element do you feel least equipped to utilize in meetings?

Tip #4: Select the Right Time Frame

- What stood out to you the most as you looked at the two meeting agenda samples?

Tip #5: Evaluate Your Meeting

Evaluate the meetings you lead:

- What do you do well?
- What could you do better?
- How happy are you with your team's level of engagement in meetings?
- How consistently does your team leave meetings with action steps they follow through on?
- What could be improved to help follow through become more consistent?

Tip #6: Use Extended Meetings on Occasion to Accelerate Outcomes

- What extended meetings do you currently use with your team?
- How would you rate those on a scale of 1–5 (1 = low; 3 = average; 5 = a model for others to follow)?
- What can you do to improve these meetings?
- What type of extended meeting do you feel you need to add to your team's annual calendar?

Put It Into Practice

Developing a new skill requires practice. Discuss with those you are training what they learned about leading meetings from their "Put It Into Practice" assignments.

1. Observe a meeting that someone else is leading, and write down the strengths and weaknesses of what you observed. Discuss what you learned from this observation experience with your trainer.

2. Write an agenda for an upcoming meeting, and send it to your trainer for review and feedback. Then lead the meeting, and invite your trainer to observe and give feedback.

3. Interview a leader who excels at leading effective and engaging meetings. Take notes, and identify two or three action steps you need to take in order to improve your own meetings. Share these with your trainer.

4. Identify a problem that needs to be solved, and plan a meeting with your team to get their input in solving the challenge. Plan specific

questions you will ask in order to increase collaboration. Afterward, evaluate the level of engagement and collaboration among the team. How effective was the meeting in identifying solutions? How well did you listen?

Reflect on Your Learning

- Where did you grow the most in this competency?
- What next step do you need to take to continue to grow in this competency?

About the Author

Mac Lake is a national consultant and training program expert whose passion is growing leaders for the local church. He was instrumental in building the church planter assessment and training process for the North American Mission Board. He has been featured in online training programs and speaks and leads seminars. Mac is the author of *The Multiplication Effect: Building a Leadership Pipeline That Solves Your Leadership Shortage*. A graduate of Moody Bible Institute and Dallas Theological Seminary, Mac and his wife Cindy live in Charleston, South Carolina. Mac blogs at maclakeonline.com and appears on Youtube at youtube.com/maclake. For more information on Mac's organization Multiply Group visit multiplygroup.org.

LET US HELP YOU TAKE YOUR NEXT STEP

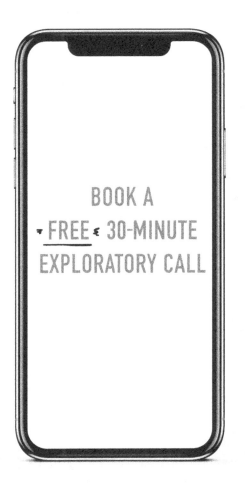

Would you like more information on how to develop leaders to take your ministry to the next level? We can help!

VISIT MULTIPLYGROUP.ORG/BOOK

CHECK OUT THE REST OF OUR
DISCIPLING LEADERS SERIES

If you want more resources like *Leading a Department*
we have books for each level of leadership in your
church or organization.

FIND MORE RESOURCES AT MULTIPLYGROUP.ORG

DISCOVER HOW TO BUILD A STRATEGY TO SOLVE YOUR LEADERSHIP SHORTAGE

The Multiplication Effect reveals a practical, biblical, and proven strategy for addressing your leadership shortage and equipping future leaders to fulfill their kingdom mission.

This book will help you:

- Identify potential leaders using unique training modules
- Equip and disciple leaders at every level of their leadership journey
- Empower leaders to multiply themselves by developing other leaders

ORDER YOUR COPY TODAY AT MULTIPLYGROUP.ORG

Made in USA - Kendallville, IN
29921_9781955142175
05.31.2024 1429